SKY RIVALS

Two Men. Two Planes.
An Epic Race around the World.

Adam L. Penenberg

WAYZGOOSE PRESS

Published in the United States by Wayzgoose Press.
Edited by Dorothy E. Zemach.
Cover and book design by DJ Rogers.

Printed in the United States.

ISBN-10: 1-938757-19-X
ISBN-13: 978-1-938757-19-8

For my Penengirls:
Charlotte, Lila, and Sophie

"The aviator, as nothing else, typifies the modern demand for annihilation of time and space. It is not enough that the schedule of the express train be cut in two; it must be halved and halved again... Speed, more speed is required, and each new advance marks the approach to the discard of the older and slower conveyances. It is bootless to inveigh against the airplane. It is here to stay, and its use will expand and swiftness increase."
—Washington Post *editorial, June 5, 1933*

"I don't want to eat. I don't want to shave. I just want to clear out of here. I flew here on tomato juice and chewing gum, and that's enough for me."
—*Wiley Post, to greeters at Templehof airport in Berlin*

"I'll see you in about a week, I hope."
—*Jimmie Mattern, to reporters, just before take-off*

Table of Contents

CHAPTER 1

Messengers from the Sky

July 1, 1931

BY 7 P.M., THE CROWD MILLING AROUND ROOSEVELT Field on Long Island had swelled to 5,000. When dusk fell an hour later, there was twice that many, a solid line of spectators crowding the half-mile fence edging the runway. A dozen planes buzzed overhead carrying sightseers and photographers. Once in a while one of them caught the attention of the onlookers, who would burst into cheers until they realized it was not the plane they were waiting for—that it was not the plane christened the *Winnie Mae.*

Virtually an entire nation eagerly awaited word of the whereabouts of Wiley Post, the one-eyed pilot from Oklahoma, and his spindly Australian navigator, Harold

Gatty, as they circled the globe in a modest single-engine airplane. For eight days, radio broadcasts, newsreels, and newspaper headlines heralded the plane's approach:

AVIATORS OVER SEA, TRYING TO GIRDLE WORLD

WORLD FLIERS FACING PERILS IN TODAY'S HOP

FLIERS WIVES HOPE THIS IS LAST STUNT

Citizens from Seattle to Savannah heaved a collective sigh of relief whenever the *Winnie Mae* touched down to refuel. Newspaper editorials lauded the airmen's courage, wrapping the dreams of a nation around the exploits of two men. Families gathered around radios. Churchgoers prayed for their safe return. Schoolteachers based geography lessons on the pilots' route as they skimmed the northern latitudes over Europe, Siberia, Alaska, and the Yukon. Meanwhile, in dusty Maysville, Oklahoma, Wiley Post's older brother Arthur ran between town and his parents' 90-acre farm with news of the *Winnie Mae's* progress, but the pilot's parents were too busy cutting hay to take much notice. "He didn't have our blessing when he started out in this flying business," groused his father to a reporter.

As the duo set to complete the 14th and final leg of their 15,474-mile journey, cruising over Canada at 150 mph, a welcoming committee formed at Long Island's Roosevelt Field, where the aviators had begun and hoped to end their journey. There were times they thought they might not make it, enduring practically everything Mother Nature could heave at them—rain so violent that Post wondered if animals might be gathering in twos below, lightning that crackled at their wingtips, crosswinds that threatened to hurl the ship into mountainsides, air so cold it iced their wings, clouds so thick that cottony mist seeped through cracks in the plane's skin.

Post and Gatty lived during the Golden Age of Aviation, when record-setting attempts were downright dangerous, perhaps foolhardy—which was why they piqued the public's imagination. In a race against space and time, reliant on temperamental technology and the whims of weather and terrain, these brave, hardy souls swept through unwelcoming skies in planes made of little more than canvas stretched over plywood, powered by 450-horsepower engines—equivalent to today's economy cars, although they propelled twice the poundage in plane, passenger, and petrol.

Mechanical breakdowns were common; Post and Gatty suffered several along the way. Radios possessed limited range; calling for help was simply not an option. Maps were unreliable, particularly in Siberia, where the two followed the tracks of the Trans-Siberian railway for long stretches. Bad weather could result in a death sentence. At times the fog and clouds forced them to travel blind: head off course a degree or two over an ocean and they risked running out of fuel with nowhere to land. Runways were often little more than stretches of sand, gravel, or mud, which could tip a craft on its nose. It was no wonder that many aerial daredevils out to set new time and distance records disappeared with nary a ripple in the vast expanse of oceans, or their bodies were crushed and seared in flaming wrecks.

Four years before Post and Gatty took to the air, a raffish young aviator named Charles A. Lindbergh had soared over the Atlantic in *The Spirit of St. Louis* and thus single-hand-edly ushered in the era of aerial conquest. Suddenly Europe wasn't another world away. It was a long day's journey into flight. The world went mad for aviation, and Lindbergh was anointed the world's most famous celebrity, recognizable to millions, the toast of two continents, an instant million-aire at a time the average wage was barely 50 cents an hour. After his return, Lindbergh toured all 48 states, and at every stop an adoring public snapped up Lindbergh china, drap-ery, shirts and towels, paperweights and pillowcases, airplane models, *Spirit of St. Louis* weather vanes. A doll bearing his likeness was a big seller at Christmas. Lindbergh had tran-scended being a man; he had become a tchotchke.

Seeking fame and fortune, other iron men in wooden planes tried to out do "Lucky Lindy." So many attempted to forge time and distance records in the days and weeks after *The Spirit of St. Louis* alighted in Paris that the time became known as the "Summer of Eagles." Two months af-ter Lindbergh hit the Champs-Élysées, Clarence Duncan Chamberlin flew 4000 miles from New York to Eisleben, Germany in 40 hours and 31 minutes. Lieutenant Dick Bently of the South African Air Force took 28 days to fly from England to South Africa. Dieudonné Costes and Joseph Lebrix skipped across the South Atlantic from Senegal to Port Natal in Brazil, and Sir Alan Cobham left England to undertake an aerial survey of Africa.

For each who succeeded, many didn't. Just be-fore Lindbergh took flight, two French aviators, Charles Nungesser and François Coli, disappeared at sea while trying to fly from Paris to the U.S. Lieutenant Roderic Carr, en route to India from England, had to be fished out of the

Persian Gulf. Walter G. Hinchliffe and Elsie Mackay disappeared somewhere over the Atlantic. In the Dole Derby, an aerial race from California to Hawaii, only two of the fourteen planes that left Oakland finished. Seven aircraft crashed; ten pilots died.

As the 1920s gave way to the 1930s, all sorts of aerial records were under assault: the first to cross the Atlantic west to east, traverse the Pacific, fly Europe to Australia, scale the North and South Poles, travel to Ireland from America, zip across the U.S. non-stop from New York to California. But only the Von Zeppelin blimp managed to circumnavigate the globe, taking 21 days.

When they set out on their epic journey, Wiley Post and Harold Gatty had been aiming to beat the "balloon." By seven p.m. on this brazenly hot Depression era day, 2000 people, each paying 25 cents admission, had swelled to 5000 and were milling around Roosevelt Field. By eight p.m., as dusk cloaked Long Island's cloud-clotted sky, 10,000 spectators lined the half a mile of fence edging the runway. One person who wouldn't make it was Jimmy Long, a ten-year old stowaway on a steamer from Boston who was desperate to brush up against history. When he docked, the boy, clad in overalls, tried some fast-talking but didn't have a ticket, and police tossed him on the next boat back.

At the airfield where the teeming crowd waited for Post and Gatty, Police Inspector Frank M. Cahill had organized a cordon of policemen, including a small battalion of motorcycle cops, their engines stuttering and spewing exhaust. Arm bands, police department passes, and ribbons identified those with an official right to be in the inner circle: the press; Mrs. Mae Post, the pilot's wife; and Dr. John H.

Finley, chairman for the Reception of Distinguished Guests; 400 people in all.

A few hundred feet away, Colonel Charles Lindbergh was parked in a limousine. After returning from Europe, Lindbergh had made commercial aviation his crusade, dedicating his life to proving that air travel was not only safe, it was the future. "America has found her wings, but she must yet learn to use them," he wrote that year. As a technical advisor to Pan American Airways, Lindbergh maintained a global vision for the company; but to span an ocean as he had done was beyond the capabilities of most men and aircraft. This led him to devise a mélange of creative solutions, each more harebrained than the others—floating runways set 300 miles apart across the Atlantic, buoys with beacons to aid in night flying, catapult takeoffs for cargo-laden planes, microfilming air mail to shave weight, blimps to float passengers from New York to London.

But Wiley Post and Harold Gatty were proving these stopgap measures would soon be unnecessary. Their success could do as much to promote aviation as Lindbergh's had. As soon as their plane landed, the police would escort Lindbergh and a small group of other VIPs to greet the fliers for a brief ceremony and then usher everyone to a nearby hangar. It was a plan that would go terribly—almost tragically—awry.

With the crowd getting antsier by the minute at Roosevelt Field, the *Winnie Mae*, Post, and Gatty crossed into Pennsylvania and were winging over the ridges of the Alleghenies. Post was short and thick, built like a piston, with untamable dark hair, a moustache, caterpillar eyebrows, and a gap between his front teeth. Gatty was of the same height, a wisp of a man who could emerge from the other side of a rainstorm as dapper as he had entered. Unlike dashing aviators such as Lindbergh and Amelia Earhart, who donned leather jackets and scarves, the two favored business suits, although theirs were rumpled and stained with oil and mud.

Both were lightheaded from gas fumes and the unwavering drone of the *Winnie Mae*'s engine. At this point they were running on little more than adrenalin. Post's leg was sore from kicking the rudder—the wooden floor pedals he used to steer the plane—and his one good eye was bloodshot from having slept only 15 hours over the past eight days. Gatty's shoulder was stiff and purple from having been whacked by the propeller in Alaska.

In contrast to the spit-and-polished Gatty, who had served in the Australian navy and was, according to Lindbergh, "the best navigator in the country, if not the world," little about Wiley Post's appearance bespoke greatness. He was squat, as if the Lord had told him this is all there was so make the best of it. Reporters described the Oklahoman pilot with the 8th grade education as "stocky," "stout," "pudgy," and "plump." In truth, Post was downright unprepossessing, and that was before he lost an eye. Only when he posed for photos, which he viewed as a formal occasion, would he pop in his glass eye. Otherwise he didn't bother, especially while flying, because at high altitudes it froze and gave him headaches. Instead he donned a white patch his wife had sewn that had become his trademark.

As Gatty liked to joke, he spoke English and Post spoke Oklahoman. It was Post's down-home persona versus Gatty's button-down starched-shirt approach to life; self-taught, fly-by-the-seat-of-your-pants versus military marching band bearing and discipline; a man who flew by feel versus one who read maps like others read newspaper comics.

Gatty was so good he could mark his location simply by looking at the sun or moon, or even by studying the flight patterns of birds. Later he would become a consultant to the U.S. Navy and pen a book for lost sailors on how to navigate without a map or compass. He tapped all these skills and more from the moment the *Winnie Mae* touched off from New York and skimmed over the Atlantic. Folded into the cramped space behind a jumble of fuel tanks, Gatty spent his time poking his sextant through a port in the roof, scribbling computations and pumping fuel into the wing tanks.

In the early 1930s, however, even the best navigators couldn't navigate without sky or horizon, and that was the *Winnie Mae's* situation halfway across the Atlantic when it rolled through a carpet of fog. "I don't think we can honestly say we were lost," Post said later, "but we just didn't know where we were." The next morning Gatty spotted an airport and Post took the plane down. "Is this England, Scotland, or Wales?" Post asked. It was Sealand Airdrome near Chester, England.

The two were right on schedule to Berlin and in and out of Moscow, but their luck turned in Siberia. Two inches of rain covered the airfield at Blagoveshchensk, and the *Winnie Mae* was trapped in mud for 14 hours until it could be rescued. But their most serious mishap occurred on day seven in Solomon, Alaska. After refueling, Post was taxiing along the beach when the wheels of the *Winnie Mae*, weighed down by 100 gallons of additional fuel, sank in the sand. He revved the engine, but all that did was push the tail up, and with a loud slap the propeller gouged a hole in the ground, bending the tips. Post cut the emergency switch just in time to keep the ship from standing on its nose, which would have spelled the end of their journey. He jumped out to survey the damage, and with a wrench, broken-handled hammer, and round stone, straightened out the blades and jumped back inside the cockpit.

Gatty yelled "All clear!" and swung the prop to restart the motor, but the engine backfired. Before he could jump out of the way, the blade spun into his shoulder. Stunned, the navigator dropped hard to the ground. He was fortunate he had been hit by the blade's flat side; otherwise, he might have been sliced in two. As it was, he twisted his back and suffered a deep bruise. After collecting his wits, Gatty climbed aboard, Post gunned the engine, and they pulled free.

That was all behind them now. Just ahead: Manhattan's skyline—the Empire State Building, completed just two months earlier, kissing the clouds; the gleaming Chrysler and majestic Flatiron buildings. The city basked in the glow of lights as day quietly retreated into evening. It was the greatest thrill of their lives. "We had gone all the way around the world for a glimpse of it from the west," Post would later say.

The first to spot the *Winnie Mae* was a Breeze monoplane once owned by Martin Jensen, one of only two pilots to have made it from Oakland to Hawaii in the Dole Derby four years earlier. Holding a cache of photographers and cameramen, the old ship might have made it to Hawaii but couldn't keep pace with the *Winnie Mae*.

Brooklyn, Jamaica, Mineola oozed into one long run-on

sentence before Post's lone bleary eye. He was floating over the Roosevelt Field hangars he had last seen eight days earlier, seeking the same spot from where they had taken off, when he spotted the crowd massing to greet them on an adjoining runway. Planes crammed the airspace above the field, and Post was anxious to land before one of them smashed into the *Winnie Mae*. Most were filled with photographers, their pilots not shy about bringing them close—too close, Post thought, wary of an in-air collision. He wondered what the photographers did with all the pictures they snapped.

"Make a turn and give them a chance," Gatty shouted through the vacuum tube they used to communicate, barely audible over the engine's rasp. "I would rather let them have it up here than made to walk the plank afterward."

Post marveled at his navigator's naiveté. Every step of their journey they had been dogged by reporters, photographers, and curiosity seekers, even in remote parts of Siberia, and the closer they got to New York, the more intense the reception. In Edmonton the crowd gave them a rousing send-off; in Cleveland well-wishers ripped Gatty's jacket pocket.

Despite adding a minute or two to their time, Post took a wide, triumphant turn for the benefit of posterity. Then, against a southeast wind, he eased in for the final approach. Extra cautious, Post stayed high over the hangars, slipped *Winnie Mae* on her left wing, and, keeping the tail down, brought the cream-white monoplane with its blue trim down to earth in a cloud of dust as the sinking sun painted the sky a gorgeous bright pink. *The New York Times* summed up the elation of an entire nation: "It was as if messengers had come out of the skies to the earth dwellers with promise of greater victories, for man has not yet come to the limit of his striving with the forces of sea and air and land."

As Post taxied up the dirt runway, flares and flash-lights blinded him as 30 policemen on motorcycles chugged through the dust to form a chain around the plane. Motion-picture trucks gunned their engines and sped toward the *Winnie Mae*. Radio announcers dragged skeins of wire, nar-rating the moment for a nationwide audience, and camera-men sprinted across the field. Suddenly a crowd of 200 a mile from the main hangars and on the opposite side of the field scaled the fence dividing the field from the old Westbury golf course and raced toward the ship. Others pushed their way through the gates.

By this time the *Winnie Mae* was a few hundred feet from the hangars. Within seconds it was under siege. Shouts of alarm mingled with cheers and screams. Hundreds of people cut through the motorcycle line, ignoring the vein-popping commands of police as they scrambled up the undercarriage, banged on the windshields, shoved, elbowed, and punched one another. Photographers set off blinding flashes. The scene reminded one reporter covering the event of several simultaneous rugby scrums.

Post, afraid the propeller might decapitate some unfor-tunate soul, cut the engine, and the blades came to a rest. His ears still ringing, Post called back to Gatty, "Well, here we are, kid." Gatty was already gone, ducking around the tail hoping to escape unnoticed—until he was chased back onboard. After Gatty put his helmet back on, Post told him, "Murderers and around-the-world fliers all have to get mugged in their working clothes."

Unable to quell the riot, Nassau County police took to cracking crania. Policemen dragged Edward Connerton from his car and beat him with billy clubs, and then charged the unarmed, 5'2" vice president of Air Services, Inc., with assault. A photographer was clubbed unconsciousness. In the heart of the melee was the 21-year-old Mae Post, afraid for her life.

Wiley Post abandoned the cockpit and jumped to the ground, his knees buckling. A policeman snatched his arm, and others used their clubs to protect him from the boisterous crowd. His petite wife, escorted to the plane by two policemen, was trembling. She had been separated from her husband for six weeks and cried as her beloved Weeley swept her into his arms and caressed her with a kiss. Before leaving her hotel to greet the plane that day, she had told reporters, "I hope he never does anything like this again."

Harold Gatty sat on the wing, eyes wide, surveying the anarchy. He was afraid Vera, his wife, might be trampled. She had tried to convince him not to go. They were raising three boys, and she'd been afraid he might not make it home. A year earlier, with Harold Bromley at the helm, Gatty had attempted the first trans-Pacific flight, which ended badly when the pilot lost his senses when carbon monoxide leaked into the cockpit. Bromley fell into spasms of laughter and put the plane into a series of wild acrobatics. Gatty couldn't decide whether to knock him out with a spanner and take over the controls or try to reason with him. Fortunately, he was able to convince Bromley to return to shore. Gatty, also poisoned by the fumes, ended up spending weeks in a hospital.

Despite the mayhem below, Gatty made a run for it and skittering through the crowd caught up to Post. As the conquering heroes were ushered to a waiting automobile, radio announcers jabbed microphones into their faces, pleading with them to say something, anything. The mob grabbed Post and Gatty, passing them shoulder-to-shoulder until the police intervened. The cops pushed the fliers into the car, locked the doors, and sealed the windows. Then the driver inched along to a nearby hangar, where more reporters awaited. Inside the air was hot and stifling, and Post and Gatty pleaded for ice water. Curiosity-seekers pushed against the hangar doors, straining to hear. Post, his tie undone and suit rumpled and grease-stained, was a sweaty mess. He sat on a car bumper until beckoned to reply to questions from Pathé News, which had paid for the exclusive first interview.

"Do you feel tired?" the reporter asked.

"Oh, not very tired," Post lied.

Actually, he was exhausted. His face was the color of week-old bread, his ears stuffed from the roar of the engine. It would take days to get his hearing back. Post tried to come to grips with how his life had changed. Consumed with planning and executing his round-the-world expedition, he hadn't given much thought to what would happen after. Practically overnight he had gone from obscure pilot to one of the most famous fliers the world had ever known.

"How do you do, Mrs. Post? What do you think of all this?"

"Wonderful," she said.

Gatty clutched a telegram from his wife that informed him her plane had been diverted to Pittsburgh by bad weather. He was relieved. This was one celebration Vera could afford to miss.

A reporter shouted, "What was the worst part of the trip?"

"This," Gatty replied, "is the worst part."

Joining the fliers in the hangar was Florence C. Hall, the crusty Oklahoman oilman who had financed the expedition, clutching his straw hat to his chest to keep it from being crushed. "What a demonstration!" he told reporters. "I knew the boys could do it."

Hall hadn't taken out insurance on the *Winnie Mae* because of the exorbitant premiums. He could have bought the plane three times over for what the insurance company wanted. For his part, Post hadn't even packed parachutes or a raft, figuring if they needed them they were doomed anyway. One VIP no longer present was Charles Lindbergh. At the first hint of trouble, he had commanded his driver to get them out of there. If there was one person who understood what Wiley Post was going through, it was Lindbergh. He'd scarcely had a moment's peace in four years.

After posing for pictures, the two fliers were whisked through the crowd of shoving men and women, some with caterwauling babes in arms, to their hotel, where they held a second press conference, and another near riot broke out. The next day they rode in a tickertape parade up Broadway, which blanketed the city in 3,000,000 pounds of confetti and was attended by more people than had seen Lindbergh or Admiral Byrd upon his return from the South Pole. At City Hall, Mayor James "Jimmy" Walker awarded them medals and told them they must have looked at the *Winnie Mae* as the "Winnie Must" when they were over Siberia and the "Winnie Did" when they landed at Roosevelt Field. They then visited the White House as honored guests of President Herbert Hoover.

Alas, today's heroes are ever at risk of becoming tomorrow's historical footnotes, their legacies as ephemeral as the vaporous trails left in their planes' wake. The day after they landed, a *Washington Post* headline declared: "Post-Gatty Record Already Menaced." Clyde "Upside Down" Pangborn and Hugh Herndon were at Roosevelt Field plotting a way to shave two days from the record. Joseph Lebrix and Martin Doret sat on a Paris runway, preparing to journey around the globe by flying to Tokyo.

But it would be a tall, charismatic Texas pilot named Jimmie Mattern who would prove to be Post's greatest rival, capturing the heart of a nation reeling from the Great Depression.

CHAPTER 2

Crack-Up Artist

JAMES J. MATTERN (EVERYONE CALLED HIM "JIMMIE") HAD been dreaming of flying around the world from the moment he took his first airplane ride. Tall, good-looking, and chatty, Mattern could win three sides of any argument. Men wanted to be like him. Women wanted to be with him. Newspapermen touted his charisma and described him as "handsome," "hulking," "barrel-chested," "broad-shouldered," "chestnut-haired" or "flaxen-haired," all while characterizing his personality as "cheerful," "friendly," "down-to-earth," and, given his accomplishments, "modest."

Mattern made for good copy, in part because he seemed to be having more fun than anyone else. He had the fortune of living during the glamour days of aviation, when those with the wherewithal to defy gravity were placed on pedestals as exotic heroes. When Mattern headed to the airport, helmet and goggles in hand and a scarf blowing gently in the breeze, traffic stopped. "Look!" people shouted. "It's an aviator!" If he buzzed a school, teachers and children rushed to the windows.

It figures the first time Mattern flew, the plane crashed. As skillful as he was, he was also lucky, and he walked away from crack-ups that would have maimed most others. He was, in fact, the greatest crash survivor of his time, something for which he would become famous. His wife got used to having him disappear in some remote area. Once, after engine trouble forced him down in the wilds of Alaska, he lived off the land for three days until he was rescued. Another time he vanished over the prairies of Texas, where he was discovered a couple of days later munching on fried chicken in a farmhouse. Then there was the time he received a telegram in Chicago inviting him to be a judge at an air race in Florida. Borrowing a plane, he started south, but plowed into an Indiana cornfield. He scrounged up another ship and this time flopped down into some Georgia sand hills. A pair of pilot pals heading in the same direction offered him a lift to Florida, where he arrived the night before the race. A friend invited Mattern to tag along to a party on a yacht, which broke down at sea. He didn't get back to shore for two days, too late to judge the race.

Jimmie Mattern was born on March 8, 1905 in Freeport, Illinois, the third of three children, two years after the Wright Brothers proved that man need not sprout wings to fly. His father had emigrated from Germany and owned a small chain of local shoe stores. Until Mattern was 15, his father and mother lived a modest middle-class existence. (The other children were much older than young Jimmie and already out of the house.) Then his father died suddenly on Memorial Day, 1920, and that changed everything. The stores were liquidated, and his mother, a housewife with no business experience, found herself with no means of support and barely enough money to last a year.

She packed up her teenaged son and they traveled to Calgary to live with his sister. Mattern dropped out of school to work and over the next year held jobs as a cowboy, limousine driver, window washer, and bus boy, but one winter of sub-zero temperatures was enough. He hopped a freight train to Seattle, with the intent of finishing school, where he met an Army recruiting sergeant.

In the Armory, sleeping in a real bed after a hearty meal was all the convincing Mattern needed. A few days shy of his 17th birthday, he lied about his age and enlisted. After boot camp, he heard about an opening in the bugle corps for a drummer—he used to drive his mother crazy drumming on walls and the furniture—and was transferred to Hawaii. There he took up the trombone and also played the bass drum in marching band and a full drum kit for concerts. He was, as he put it, "a scrawny, know-nothing eighteen-year-old Army kid in Oahu" who liked to idle away hours near Pearl Harbor watching aircraft take off and land. A 2nd lieutenant pointed to the sky at an approaching ship and told Mattern, "When that plane, up there, comes down I am going to take it up and wring it out."

"Can I go with you?" Mattern asked.

They taxied a short distanced, and the Curtiss Jenny, an open cockpit biplane that was one of the most popular air vessels of its day, lifted off. When they hit 150 feet in altitude the propeller quit and they fell into a sugar cane field. Mattern was thrown but not seriously hurt. He joined the crowd gathering around the wreck, watching good Samaritans attempt to extract the lieutenant. Someone said, "There were two fellows in that plane. Where is the other guy? He must be tangled in the wreckage and probably dead now."

"I'm the other one who was in that plane," Mattern said, and promptly fainted. He and the lieutenant were taken to the hospital and soon released with minor cuts and scratches.

In those days, plane crash survivors were immediately taken back up in the air so they wouldn't develop a fear of flying. That night, Mattern flew in an old Keystone bomber, up front in the plane's transparent nose, peering down on Oahu's lights. It was a breathtaking sight. Right there and then, Mattern decided he wanted to become a pilot. In 1925, after his three-year military service was up, he was honorably discharged and given $300. Once again he ended up in Seattle, and organized a jazz band to perform on a tourist ship to Alaska and another to the Orient.

When he returned, Mattern thirsted for greater adventures. He applied for the Air Corps but was rejected, which only made him more determined. The Corps was the West Point of the air, and, on average, of 300 cadets admitted, only 65 graduated. The cadets who made it through became career officers and built the modern Air Force. Those who didn't make the grade learned to fly elsewhere, picking up World War I surplus planes called "Jennys" and barnstorming, creating small, local airlines and establishing grass field airports. They were just as much pioneers of aviation.

The following year, Mattern married his girlfriend, Delia, a pretty, curly-haired blonde whose family hailed from Walla Walla, Washington. But after the honeymoon, Mattern didn't stick around long. Just 22 years old, he couldn't fight the lure of being a pilot.

He took his savings and traveled to Ryan Aircraft in San Diego, California. The factory had just received an order from a young barnstorming pilot named Charles Lindberg preparing for a non-stop solo flight from New York to Paris. The place was fast becoming a hotbed of aviation, with would-be pilots like Mattern flocking there to learn to fly.

Aviation was so young that Mattern's instructor, who had logged barely 500 hours in the air, was considered a grizzled veteran. The instructor took him up in a surplus Jenny and showed him the basics over the sandy field at Dutch Flats, which was marked by 1500 feet of high-tension wire on the approach side. After three hours and 20 minutes, Mattern was soloing. "No matter what you have done in flying, even though it is basic, the biggest thrill of all is the first time you find yourself up there all alone," Mattern reflected decades later. "The instructor is no longer in that front cockpit. It's a once in a lifetime feeling. You never had it before but you have it now. All by yourself, life or death."

He hopped the train to Troy, Ohio, and plunked down cash he had saved for a Waco 10, a three-seat open cockpit biplane similar to the Jenny. When the Waco factory representative found out how inexperienced Mattern was, he refused to let him fly it home and lined up pilot Freddie Lund to chauffeur him back west. "Fearless Freddie" Lund was a legendary silent movie stunt pilot and wing-walker for the Gates Flying Circus, the "greatest show on earth" in the Twenties, who had performed the first loop ever done in a commercial airplane. With Mattern as his passenger, he navigated over the Midwest and through New Mexico to California by following railroad tracks, which he called "the iron compass."

Lund stuck around Los Angeles, where Mattern had just moved to; they both figured any guy with good looks and his own plane was sure to find work. The veteran pilot showed his young, eager charge his full arsenal of tricks, and Mattern was officially a pilot now, assigned license number 250, signed by none other than Orville Wright. Four decades later, astronaut Buzz Aldrin would pay tribute to Mattern by carrying his pilot's license with him to the moon and back.

After his lessons ended, Mattern learned that a motion picture called *Lilac Time* was about to begin shooting. The next day Mattern flew to a field near Santa Ana that had been transformed into a war-time airport with hangars, pilots' quarters, and other weather-beaten buildings. He put on a show, figuring he'd audition with a few moves Lund had shown him. With the air clear of ships, Mattern uncorked a series of snap rolls, power dives, wingovers, loops, and barrel rolls, the power of the engine urging him on to wilder and wilder acrobatics. He ended the impromptu show with a power dive and then hung his ship by its propeller until transitioning into a soft landing. He was offered a job on the spot.

His first mission was particularly dangerous. Lofting above the clouds, he started a 5000-foot power dive with two other pilots through a bomber formation consisting of more than 50 planes, a tactic made famous by the Red Baron in the Great War. His motor running full throttle, Mattern followed the other planes as they slipped through a narrow slit in the formation. He had to fight the controls as he battled the wash of the pursuit planes and pack of bombers, and felt sick when he frantically pulled out of the dive as the ground rushed toward him.

After he landed, the other pilots congratulated him, and the cameraman reported the dive was a dream: a one-take stunt. Although he felt like he had aged ten years in ten minutes, Mattern knew he was going to like stunt flying, and a few weeks later was hired for another film: *Hell's Angels*, produced by an enigmatic millionaire by the name of Howard Hughes.

Mattern's duties for Hughes consisted of stunt flying for the film, shuttling the stars to and from the set, and crash-testing prototypes Hughes' company worked on, including a Thomas Morris Scout, which sported a Rotary Le Rhone engine that rotated with the propeller. Mattern took it up to 5000 feet and put it through every maneuver he could think of, slicing through clouds and banking hard left. When he banked steeply right, the ship spun out and Mattern barely recovered. After landing, he said, "Howard, whatever you do up there, do not bank too steeply to the right. The airplane might snap into a spin."

Mattern was skeptical of Hughes' flying ability—he had even fewer hours in the air than Mattern did—but no one told Howard Hughes what to do. He taxied down the runway and started his ascent. Mattern strolled over to a fence to watch. Less than 200 feet up, Hughes banked steeply to the right and the plane spun in. Mattern was over the fence just as Hughes hit the ground. He pulled Hughes out of the ship before it caught fire. Although the plane was totaled, Hughes emerged with only a large gash on his forehead. An hour later, he was back on the set, a bandage wrapped around his head, shouting, "On with the show!"

For the movie, Mattern flew through open barns, carried wing walkers, and flew under the Pasadena Bridge near the Rose Bowl, which made the newspapers. If the director wanted clouds for a more realistic effect, Mattern sometimes found himself flying blind through overcast skies, completely discombobulated. On top of thick cloud cover, sometimes skimming mountaintops, was not the place to stick your nose when other planes and pilots were equally blind. At least, he reasoned, the hayfields that dotted the countryside would be suitable for emergency landings.

Mattern quickly found himself hooked on the adrenaline, experiencing equal parts fear and excitement. The notoriously tricky and unforgiving vintage WWI planes required constant adjustments and absolute concentration, particularly in low-level flight and tight formation. After a couple of hours of reshoots, the pilots' clothes were soaked in sweat, their arms sore and their heads aching from the drone of the engines and the stress of living on the edge of oblivion. Then they had to go right back up again.

Mattern wasn't one to court danger if he could avoid it, sometimes crafting creative ways around it. In one film, the stunt coordinator wanted a pilot to land at high speed and send a plane crashing between two trees. None of the established fliers was eager for the assignment, so Mattern volunteered. That night he enlisted the assistance of the prop department and ordered lifelike paper wings attached to an old plane body. The following morning, Mattern took his plane up and landed right in front of the camera. As soon as the wheels touched down, he gunned the engine, barely lifting the ship over the trees. Then he jumped into the doctored plane and taxied between the trees, where the wings ripped off realistically. The stunt coordinator was livid. He had paid $300 for a dangerous stunt, yet admitted the melding of the two shots yielded the memorable movie moment he had envisioned.

On the set, life was cheap, and the pilots often promised that a particularly hair-raising stunt would be their last. For one segment, the stunt coordinator approached Mattern to fly a Sikorsky S-29A bomber repainted to look like a WWI German Gotha, which would be shot down in flames and spin out of control. Both Dick Grace and Frank Clarke, top stunt pilots of their day, wouldn't even attempt it for less than $10,000. They had flown the bomber that morning and were convinced no pilot could pull it out of a spin. Although the stunt coordinator pleaded, raved, and threatened, Mattern added his refusal to the rest.

Eventually veteran pilot Pete Wilson stepped forward, and Phil Jones, a young mechanic, volunteered to operate the machine that would blow black smoke from the diving plane. Then Mattern and the rest of the stunt squadron were ordered into their ships for the dogfight that would send the bomber to its doom. As the stunt coordinator walked away, Mattern said he hated to wash out on him. "Listen here, Jimmie," another pilot told him. "You're no cat, my boy—you've got only one life and it's yours—nobody else's. Now let's go up and start dog fighting. That's a nice peaceful way to risk our necks."

On March 22, 1929, Wilson took the Sikorsky up to 7500 feet, trailed by three camera planes to record its every move. Mattern joined 30 other pilots in their planes, propellers churning the air and motors yielding a cacophony of high, snarling pitches. The ships twisted and turned in an intricate choreography, catching the glint of sun on their wings, machine guns yammering. On cue, the great black bomber staggered, hesitated, and its nose dropped toward the earth.

Mattern unleashed a burst of fake fire at the "enemy" and then zoomed out of the way, watching the bomber's flight path. It started to spin, slowly at first and then faster and faster as it plunged to earth. From the rear of the ship came a column of black smoke, courtesy of the boy stationed in the tail. Mattern could see fabric tearing away from the left wing, with pieces of cowling from the left engine beginning to break away. He realized the spinning bomber was hopelessly out of control. There was the white puff of an opening parachute, which meant the pilot had wisely bailed. Mattern scanned the sky for another parachute. It never came.

He watched the plane smack down on one wing, bounce high in the air, and then turn over on the other wing, desecrating the earth. It came to rest in a cloud of dust. Little dots that were men rushed to the wreckage, but Mattern knew there was no hope. Later he learned the plane had crashed with the young man's parachute still strapped to his body. The three aerial cameras were still recording, so he swallowed, steadied his hand, and dove once more into the thick of the dog fight, until he got the all clear signal to break off the attack.

Waiting with the other pilots for the next shot, Mattern sat out of the sun in a shed that had been converted into pilots' quarters. They were a gloomy, dispirited bunch. One of the older fliers said, "He didn't have a chance in the world, stuck in the tail of that ship. It's what I've been telling you guys for weeks. You're crazy to stick in this business. Plain crazy! Every time something like this happens, I swear I'm getting out. And the next day I'm back up again, flyin' these junks around—Snipes. Sopwiths, a bunch of absolute junk. Flyin' war time coffins when there isn't even a war goin' on."

It was true, Mattern realized. He couldn't think of stunt pilot who had walked away from Hollywood with his body in one piece and a bankroll stuffed in his pocket. The week before, one of the men had torn the wings off an old Fokker, barely getting out alive—and what happened? He had to do it again because of the sun's glare on the camera lens. Retakes—on your life. Pain and broken bones if not death awaited them, all for money that mysteriously vanished during weeks they were not employed. Three men had died during the filming of *Hell's Angels*. Mattern wondered if he would be next, but he had signed a contract and promised to see it through to the end.

On the ground, however, life was not only safer, it was downright festive, and befriending a millionaire had its advantages. Mattern and Hughes were close in age and had become fast friends, often double dating, with Mattern neglecting to tell Hughes about his wife back home in Washington. Hughes cast starlets based on how badly he wanted to sleep with them, and let it be known that he was a "tits and ass man."

At the time, Hughes was on a Dusenberg kick—he owned six of them. When Mattern spied a Roll Royce covered in dust on a back lot, a little of Hughes' audacity rubbed off on him. He took on an air of authority to order around a maintenance man. "Get Mr. Hughes' Rolls Royce out and clean it up," he shouted. "Have it ready for driving. I will pick it up this afternoon." Mattern couldn't believe it worked, and drove it around Hollywood for months. He didn't have the money to take dates to fancy restaurants, but most didn't seem to care. "It wasn't the most comfortable for making love," Mattern said, "but what car is?"

He took it to work one day while Hughes was standing at the entrance.

"I don't pay you enough for you to own your own Rolls Royce," Hughes said. "Where did you get the car?"

"Howard, it's your car."

"It is? Put it back where you got it."

The "Hollymoon," as Mattern put it, was over.

When the Depression hit, the banks closed and unemployment topped 25 percent, Mattern found himself barely able to scratch out a living. He carted frozen seafood over the Gulf of Mexico, once almost colliding head on with Charles Lindbergh flying in the opposite direction, and signed on as the personal pilot for a rich wildcat oilman before becoming chief pilot for Cromwell Airlines, which operated in Texas and Oklahoma.

Like almost everyone else, Mattern keenly followed Wiley Post and Harold Gatty's progress in 1931 as they became the first aviators to circumnavigate the world. But an aerial expedition like that took money—lots of it—and time. Mattern was too busy hopping from one southwest dust trap to another, ferrying packages and people.

After Carl Cromwell died in an auto accident and the company went belly up in 1932, Mattern ended up with one of the planes. As luck would have it, it was a Lockheed Vega, the same make and model that Wiley Post and Amelia Earhart flew. And Mattern saw his chance. Before he could smash aerial records, however, Mattern needed a way to pay for fuel and maintenance. Like many Americans, he had lost all his savings when his bank shuttered its doors. Mattern stored his Vega in a Ft. Worth hangar and joined the Air Corp Reserve, not only to keep his flying skills sharp but for the three square meals a day.

As fate would have it, his roommate was Bennett H. Griffin, a relentlessly pleasant former World War I flying ace who was, it must be said, best known for turning back two hours into the Oakland to Hawaii Dole Derby when his engine overheated, forcing him to limp back to Oakland. Griffin considered himself lucky. Out of ten planes six crashed and two disappeared over the Pacific. Only two teams made it to Hawaii.

Critics claimed Griffin lacked nerve, a criticism that cut deep. Mattern thought it was wholly unjust. Griffin was one of the coolest pilots he'd ever met. Wiley Post agreed. He and Griffin, both fellow Oklahomans, often ran into one another, but Post never participated in the razzing Griffin endured. He was a war hero who had seen his share of death. When he returned after the Armistice, Griffin locked himself in a room for a week, wondering if, after all the aerial carnage he had wrought, that he should even be a pilot anymore.

As Mattern showed off his Lockheed Vega, Griffin suggested they fly to Hawaii. This had already been done, so Mattern told him to think bigger. "Benny," he asked, "how would you like to be my partner in an attempt to break the around-the-world speed record?" After all, Lockheed had a motto: "It takes a Lockheed to beat a Lockheed," which originated from a 1930 air race between Chicago and Los

Angeles, when Wiley Post in his Lockheed Vega edged out by eleven seconds another aerial legend, Art Goebel, who flew the same make and model—in fact, it was Post's old plane. Why not, Mattern said, take a Lockheed to beat a Lockheed to beat a Lockheed?

It took them ten minutes to agree and more than ten months to raise money, gain corporate sponsors, secure visas, and customize the plane. Sparing no expense, they installed ice detectors, a Richie compass, and communications devices consisting of an internal telephone connection and a tube through which they could pass notes in a small aluminum bucket. The improvements ran roughly $50,000, a fortune in 1932 when the average annual per capita income was $750 and more than half of Americans were living below subsistence levels.

Mattern and Griffin spent a week at the Air Corps training center at Randolph Field in Texas to learn to fly by instrument so they could fly blind, if need be. At the time, conventional wisdom held that a pilot could not fly by instruments for more than an hour without losing equilibrium and tumbling out of the sky. Over the Atlantic Ocean, however, the water acts as a mirror, reflecting the sky, so that both water and atmosphere appear as a solid sheet of color. From the point of view of the pilot, there is no horizon, no up or down.

The plane toted 450 gallons of fuel, weighing more than a ton, much of it in the wing-mounted barrels Wiley Post had loaned them. Mattern asked Post this favor because they owned identical planes, so the tanks could be attached without any customization. Amelia Earhart said, "It was just like Wiley to let them take the extra tanks out of his plane and put them in their Lockheed." Harold Gatty donated navigation advice, maps, and charts, recommending that Mattern and Griffin stick to Post and Gatty's original route, hugging the earth's northernmost latitudinal rings. All were rivals, of course, yet they belonged to the same informal club of pilots pushing boundaries. It would never have occurred to any of them not to help the others.

Along the way Mattern and Griffin almost plowed into an ocean liner as they skimmed the ocean's surface to undercut thick fog, and they got lost over Newfoundland and outside of Berlin, where a crowd of people assembled in a makeshift arrow to point their way to Templehof Airport. Nevertheless they managed to break the trans-Atlantic record set earlier that year by Amelia Earhart, and were well ahead of Post and Gatty's time as they crossed into Russia from Poland.

"Benny," Mattern messaged to his co-pilot, "if everything goes well, we should be able to make the entire trip around the world in less than five days"—beating the record by more than three and a half days.

Then, 50 miles from Minsk, disaster struck. After so many hours of constant vibration, the hatch broke loose and shot into the cockpit, shredding their control panel and nearly decapitating Mattern, hurtling back against the tail of the ship and pulverizing the vertical fin.

Mattern struggled to keep the plane level as gasoline sloshed heavily in the tanks. With so much flammable liquid, he was piloting a giant flying bomb. Below, cast in moonlight, was a field blotted with haystacks. He banked around and throttled down, gently gliding the plane down on the edge of the field. The plane rolled so smoothly Mattern congratulated himself on a perfect landing. He figured they would be able to repair the damage and soon be on their way. A split second later, the wheels sank through the earth's crust and the airplane pirouetted on its nose. Mattern revved the engine hoping to break free, but the plane remained vertical, frozen awkward in time, and then flipped on its roof.

After a dizzying half-second, Mattern was flat on his back, trapped in his seat, straddling the motor that burned his knees. Through the open hatch Mattern's hair was touching the ground. The fuel tanks had ruptured and gas was streaming down his neck. With the engines hot, he was afraid he was about to become a living torch.

Never having been upside down in a safety belt before, he was having trouble figuring out how to escape. He heard Griffin outside the plane.

"Well, Jimmie," he drawled, "what ocean is this?"

Mattern told him about the gas.

"Oh, there's plenty of gas," Griffin said, always the joker. "How's your oil pressure?"

Mattern flicked the safety buckle and found his head half-buried in peat bog. He shimmied and got his belly down, but the ground covered the hatch and he was trapped. Griffin dug frantically, reminding Mattern of a dog going after a bone. Soon Mattern was able to stick one foot through the hole, then the other. Griffin grabbed his ankles and yanked. Twisted metal from the broken hatch sliced into Mattern's back and shoulders while sharp rocks in the bog cut him from his knees to his face, until he emerged on the other side. The rescue hurt more than the accident.

Griffin was in worse shape. A five-gallon fuel can had left a deep gash in his forehead. Mattern stumbled into the bog to retrieve their medical kit, which had been thrown clear of the ship. He fumbled for the iodine and poured it over his friend's cut. Griffin screamed obscenities. The sun was rising, and Mattern could see the plane was broken into two and lying upside down. He wiped away tears, his spirit nearly as crushed as the plane's fuselage. While lucky to be alive, his disappointment was almost too much to bear.

After the engines cooled and the danger of fire passed, they crawled on the wing and lay there, administering to their wounds. They figured that as soon as dawn broke they wouldn't be alone for long, and they were right. A platoon of armed soldiers surrounded them, poking bayonets into their chests and shouting in Russian. For several hours Mattern and Griffin remained prisoners on the wing of the wrecked plane, unable to communicate. Finally a Soviet General appeared, trailed by a pack of reporters who had been waiting for the two fliers at the airport in Moscow.

Mattern and Griffin were placed under house arrest and confined to a Minsk hotel. A few days later they were transferred to Moscow, where they were intermittently feted at banquets with caviar and champagne then returned to their hotel rooms with only dried fish to eat. Before a military tribunal in the Kremlin they were accused of spying, questioned for a day and a half, then suddenly informed they were free to go. The authorities helped them cart up the wreckage and send it home, while the two of them returned to America via Europe, stopping in several capitals along the way as tourists. Waiting for them at home was an invitation from President Herbert Hoover to visit the White House. "They were making wonderful time and it's too bad they had to crash," Wiley Post told an Associated Press reporter.

Mattern's mother told a niece that when "your Uncle Jimmie gets back this time, we're going to tie a ball and chain to him so he can't ever get away again."

But Mattern would have none of that. He vowed to try again, alone, just as soon as he could scrounge up a plane.

CHAPTER 3

One-Eyed Ace

WILEY HARDEMAN POST WAS MORE AT EASE AROUND machinery than men. Machines he could fix—one look at a wheat thresher or car engine and he knew exactly how it worked and why it wasn't. With people, though, he never knew what they wanted. Whenever forced to address a crowd, the best he could do was mumble a few platitudes and skulk away. At home his wife did most of the talking, "and I don't talk that much," she said.

To his friends, he was simply "Weeley": warm to friends, cool to strangers, and given to sudden mood shifts, from bouts of sweetness to squalls of anger. He dressed in the dark to avoid waking his wife and had a soft spot for children. Perhaps his greatest disappointment was that he and his wife never had kids. He could be irascible with government bureaucrats who sometimes gummed up his plans and short-tempered with reporters who did their utmost to get him to say something, anything, interesting. Rarely did he oblige. He flew planes and tinkered with cars, liked hunting and fishing, and the two things he collected were guns and wristwatches, giving away the guns to friends and hoarding the watches, which he'd wind and set to the exact time before every trip.

Racing through clouds, however, Post was transformed. As one of his students put it, "He didn't just fly an airplane, he put it on." Up there in the clouds Post was a bold risk taker with a need for speed; a pilot, it was said, who could land on a mountain peak. Those who knew him were as impressed with his piloting skill as his sheer courage. "He apparently didn't have a nerve in his body," said a businessman who had flown with him on numerous occasions. "When other people were scared, Wiley just grinned." Another pilot claimed that Post made cross-country hops without even looking at a compass or a map, flying strictly by feel, as if it were the most natural thing in the world. His takeoffs could be flashy, almost vertiginous. From a near standing start he would shoot almost straight up and then bank right, so he could see out of his good eye.

Once, while attempting an altitude record, he glided down 30,000 feet after his engine conked out, performing a perfect "dead stick" landing in the Mojave Desert. Sealed in a pressurized suit of his own design, he staggered out of the ship and over to a stranded motorist whose engine had overheated. The man's head was under the hood, and when Post tapped him on the shoulder he looked up and screamed. He thought Post was from Mars and aliens were attacking. Post had to tackle him before the man calmed down enough to help him out of the suit and walk with him to a telegraph station for help.

Born on a Texas farm on November 22, 1898, Post came from a hardscrabble background. His sister Mary, born when Wiley was three, became the pet of the family, and his older brother received preferential treatment. That left the young Wiley pretty much alone, both in the house and on the farm. Nobody seemed to care much what he did as long as he took care of a few simple chores each day. When he was a boy the talk at the family dinner table revolved around the discovery of oil on Indian territory. It seemed everyone they knew was moving to Oklahoma to sink life savings into land leases near oil fields, which made land elsewhere more affordable and enabling his father, William Francis Post, to purchase 320 acres of farmland in Abilene, Texas.

A larger farm meant more machinery. Post never forgot the first time he laid eyes on a harvester. His father and older brother poured over the instruction manuals, squirting oil on various bearings, and Post remembered the clicking sounds from the copper squirt can decades later. He was so enamored with the machine that they had to shoo him away from the blades. Before he was five he knew the harvester's every function.

The family moved again, to Chickasha, Oklahoma, when Post was eight. Life continued to be hard, both on the farm, where his father was barely able to keep his homestead afloat, and at home. His family treated Post as if he were an afterthought. He was short for his age, shy, unassuming, and did poorly in school, unlike his oldest brother Jim, who excelled. Another son, Gordon, was born, and the family relocated to Maysville, Oklahoma, where Post began to flex his independence by earning money as a door-to-door mechanic. As an 11- and 12-year-old-boy, he repaired sewing machines and lubricated farm equipment, tweaked gas generators, and sharpened reaper blades. By the time he was 13 he dropped out of school.

In 1913, Maysville was agog with the upcoming county fair in Lawton, where an "aëroplane ascent" was advertised as part of the show. Post "hornswoggled" his father into letting him go, provided he agreed to extra chores and pay admission for his older brother, Jim. Setting out after dusk with the family's horse and buggy, they arrived at the fairgrounds the following morning after a 50-mile journey. They found a place to hitch the horse and the two brothers split up, with Post making a beeline for the farm machinery—the new plows, tractors, and reapers in dazzling red and blue. He never made it.

Alone in a field was the oddest-looking contraption Post had ever seen. He figured it must be that "aëroplane" he had been hearing about. Post couldn't take his eyes off it. Later he would learn it was an old Curtiss pusher. "To this day I have never seen a bit of machinery for land, sea, or sky that has taken my breath away as did that old pusher," he said. Post spent the entire morning and afternoon with it, measuring the height in "hands" just like he had seen his father do with horses. That evening Post was sitting in the rickety cockpit when his brother found him. He was two hours late meeting Jim at the hitching post. Post had even neglected to feed and water the horse; luckily his brother had taken care of it.

This was a special day for another reason. On the way home, while Post was taking the reins from his brother, a "gas buggy" passed, scaring their horse. Up to then he and his brother had only seen automobiles in magazine ads, and if the exhausted nag hadn't walked 80 miles over the last day and a half, she might have bolted. Ten miles later they came upon the car stuck in a ditch. The driver asked for help, but the horse wouldn't go anywhere near the automobile. Post offered to fetch help in exchange for $1 and a ride home in the car. His brother dropped him off at a nearby sawmill and continued to the farm while Post convinced the mill owner and three workers to help pull the car out of the ditch.

Post got his ride, passing Jim about a mile from the farm. The car again spooked the horse, and Jim shook his fist at them. Post couldn't help but laugh along with the driver. "The machine age was coming; I knew it," Post recounted later. After this, his fascination with all things mechanical grew. He equipped the farm with a gasoline engine to pump water, and by creating a series of belts, made it work as a mechanical jack-of-all trades: a corn sheller, grindstone, buzz saw; anything to make the farm run more efficiently.

By 1916, Post was 17 and had grown as tall as he ever would: five feet, five inches. He had a freckly moon face topped with uncooperative dark hair. Post worked out a deal with his father to sharecrop a ten-acre plot of land where he raised cotton in exchange for a portion of the profits. It was backbreaking work, but he earned the $85 he needed to enroll at the Sweeney Auto School, one of the first of its kind.

The following year the United States entered the World War, and Post joined the Students' Army Training Camp, where he studied radio, math, and chemistry. His brothers were fighting in Europe, and Post expected he would join them when he turned 18. He hoped the Army would train him to fly, and in his spare time he hung around the local military airport, watching the planes come and go. Just as he was set to graduate, the war ended.

Instead of Europe, Post found himself in Walters, Oklahoma, earning $7 a day as a handy man at an oil field "rasslin' iron" and "firing pots": feeding boilers, threading pulleys, and transporting spare parts 12 hours a day. There was nothing to spend money on in the fields, so he soon found himself with a healthy stake, which Post tried to parlay into a small fortune.

He tried his hand as a wildcatter, purchasing a small piece of land and searching for oil, but came up empty. Broke, he found work as a driller, saved a tidy bundle, bought more land, and failed again. Then the price of oil dipped and people were reluctant to lease land for drilling. Post's savings evaporated. Worse, he couldn't find a job.

Desperate, he resorted to armed robbery. He set up a barricade on a quiet country road and when a car stopped, he pulled a gun on the driver. There was a spate of these heists over the course of months, until Post stopped the wrong car and was overpowered by four men. He was arrested, tried, convicted, and sentenced to ten years in the State Reformatory in Granite, Oklahoma. Locked in a cell, he fell into a deep depression. Post refused to speak, wouldn't eat. He was diagnosed with a "melancholic" state that "was steadily growing worse."

On June 5, 1922, after Post had served 13 months in prison, Oklahoma governor J.B.A. Robertson signed his parole papers. Post was required to abstain from liquor—he didn't drink anyway—couldn't gamble, had to avoid "evil associations, improper places of amusement, all pool and billiard halls, obey the laws," and "industriously follow some useful occupation." The rest of his life he lived in fear that his secret criminal past would come to light and he would lose everything.

Post returned to the oil fields, but one day on a drilling job near Holdenville, Post saw a plane overhead and the urge to fly swept over him again. He quit the business right there and headed for a little town called Wewoka, Oklahoma, where a flying circus had decamped. The three men in charge possessed two beaten, battered planes. The parachutist had taken three jumps that week, but slightly injured himself on the fourth. Post volunteered to make the next jump even though he had never before been in a plane.

The next day Post found himself in the sky, 2000 feet up. The pilot cut the throttle and shouted, "O.K., get ready!" Forgetting everything he had been told, Post peered at the pilot, who replied with a glare. Post threw a leg over the side and inched his way to the wing's edge. He buckled his harness to the snap rings of the parachute and dropped to his knees. The pilot turned the ship to get into position over the drop zone, pointed to his right, and yelled, "Let's go!" Post backed off the wing and swung helplessly underneath. He hung there for several seconds until he remembered to pull the release cord.

He fell. Air whooshed by his ears. Then he felt a sharp tug as the chute opened. He looked down and had one of the biggest thrills of his life. The people below looked like ants on a well-worn rug. Soon he realized he was off course, heading for a field. When he hit, his knees buckled. He tried to run the way he had been told but fell flat on his face. But he made it.

The following week he jumped again and earned $50. Soon he became a regular jumper with the Burrell Tibbs Flying Circus. A few months later, Post went into business for himself. "Town boosting" was the order in Oklahoma communities in 1924, and Post was able to enlist Chamber of Commerce and Rotary Club members to stage parachute jumps on Sundays for up to $200 a jump. For $25 or less, Post could hire a plane and pilot and the rest he kept. He didn't care how bad a piece of junk the plane (or pilot) was. All he cared about was that it could get him a couple thousand feet above over the fairgrounds. Post was his own actor, manager, and bookkeeper.

Once he jumped over an audience of farmers and their horses and buggies, sailing down until he ended up on one side of a mule with the parachute draped over the other. Spooked by the uninvited passenger, the animal bolted, dragging Post and the parachute behind. Post bumped and rolled as the mule sprinted past shocked onlookers until he managed to uncouple himself and roll to a halt. Without missing a beat he jumped to his feet to give chase. That was a new parachute, and there was no way he was going to lose it.

He returned to Maysville and organized a jump through the Chamber of Commerce, offering a hometown discount: $75. But the reunion with his family, whom he hadn't seen in two years, was disappointing. When his father learned how he earned a living, he tried to persuade his son to quit. They argued almost every minute Post was on the farm. The day before the jump, Post discovered his parachute missing. He checked closets, bedrooms, the barn, and the outhouse, but it was nowhere to be found. Post postponed the event and took the train to Oklahoma City to borrow a parachute. Then he stayed with the pilot in a nearby town until the big day. After the plane circled Maysville a few times, and the pilot performed some loops and a slow roll, Post leaped and landed in the exact spot he said he would. Even his father was impressed.

Post spent two years barnstorming, jumping almost 200 times by his own count under several aliases, including "The Flying Redskin," a nod less to his one-eighth Cherokee heritage than to his appearance. Eventually the business stagnated. Airplanes weren't the rarity they had once been and were becoming commonplace. Post knew his barnstorming days were coming to an end. If he wanted to live his life in the sky, he had to become a pilot. To do that, he needed to buy his own plane, and that took money. In December 1925, a new oil field at Seminole opened, and Post returned to the dirty business of drilling.

Once again fate intervened. On October 1, 1926, a roughneck was pounding a bolt with a sledgehammer when a shard of metal struck Post in the eye. Post was transported to a hospital where he lay in complete darkness for several days. When the bandages were removed, he could make out shapes and light with his right eye but nothing with his left. Worse, the infection was spreading, a symptom known as sympathetic ophthalmia.

After doctors amputated the eyeball, Post stayed with an uncle in southwest Texas to convalesce. As the sight in his right eye gradually returned, Post worked on depth perception. He would look at a hill or tree and estimate how far he stood from it and then step off the distance, his four-mile-per-hour gait acting as a guide. At first his calculations were way off; little by little they improved until he was better at it with one eye than most were with two. Meanwhile, the Oklahoma Industrial Court awarded Post $1,800 in workman's compensation, which he used to purchase a used Canuck that had been in a slight crash. The owners couldn't afford to repair it, so Post purchased it for $240 and invested another $300 in having it rebuilt. "I bought a plane," Post said, "but it cost me an eye."

Months after his first flying lesson, Wiley Post was soloing with a passenger onboard: Mae Laine of Sweetwater, Oklahoma, his 17-year-old fiancée. The Laine family was against the courtship. Her parents didn't approve of Post's peripatetic lifestyle. He was a one-eyed pilot without a steady job, and they were concerned about the 11-year age difference.

On June 27, 1927, a month after Lindbergh had crossed the Atlantic, Post and his bride-to-be were on their way to tell her family of their decision to marry. They climbed into Post's plane for the Laine farm, but a faulty distributor rotor led to engine failure, and he landed in a farmer's field near Graham, Oklahoma. With no way to reach the Laine house before nightfall, there was only one thing to do: locate a justice of the peace. Once married, they spent the next two days overhauling the faulty part and sleeping on a wooden oilrig platform. The difference in their ages was a source of amusement to Post, who joked that he had raised Mae. "I'd tell him to stop," Mae Post once recalled, "because people might believe him."

Meanwhile, Post set out to earn a living as a pilot, flying businessmen in his rickety open cockpit plane to oil fields and toting packages and freight from Oklahoma outposts to towns and beyond. He often encountered mechanical difficulty. Jack Baskin, a former classmate of Post's at the Sweeney Auto School, recalled working on his ship at the Ponca City airport when he saw a plane fall into a nearby field of wheat. He drove to the crash site and out stepped Wiley Post neck high in wheat. "Broke my oil line," he explained. Baskin helped Post tape the pipe and crank the motor, but after three tries it was apparent there wasn't enough space to lift off. Suddenly a farmer with a shotgun came running at them. While Baskin jumped into his car, Post gunned the motor and barely managed to get his wings clear of the fields. That was how, as legend has it, Post learned to take off from a near a standing start.

He encountered other troubles, too. There was talk that all pilots would need licenses. Afraid his ocular disability would disqualify him, Post flew his rust bucket of a plane across Oklahoma and North Texas, careful to land at out-of-the-way airfields that didn't bother to check his credentials, or to deplane after dusk in the hopes that airport officials would have by then gone home. It was tough going. He and his newlywed wife moved into a small apartment in Oklahoma City and barely made ends meet. After another minor crash, Post couldn't afford repairs. Desperate for work, he approached F.C. Hall, a rich Oklahoman oilman, to see if he'd be interested in employing a full-time pilot.

Florence C. Hall was working at a Texas drugstore when oil fever swept the region, and parlayed a $250 stake into a fortune. He possessed an almost supernatural ability to find oil where others found rocks and dirt. Over a decade he had drilled 300 gushers and only two dusters. Hall didn't need much convincing that he could use a pilot. He traveled around Oklahoma to check on new drilling sites, and had recently missed out on a deal because he couldn't get there fast enough. He offered Post a salary of $200 a month, and although his wardrobe was in dire need of improvement, he took his first paycheck and bought a hunting rifle. Hall told Post to buy an airplane, a three-seat Travelair, which they crammed with up to five people and their luggage.

Hall had one condition: Post had to earn his pilot's license. He helped Post wrangle a waiver for his ocular disability, although he had to sit for an eight-hour written exam, which he passed. But Post had never kept a flight log, so he couldn't show how many hours he had in the air. As a result the state examiners required him to put in 800 flying hours, which he did over the next seven months. Post received license number 3259 from the Aeronautics Branch of the United States Department of Commerce. Like Jimmie Mattern's, it was signed by Orville Wright.

Post impressed his new employer with his piloting skill. While in Hall's open cockpit plane once, they were caught in a violent squall over the Texas Panhandle. The small craft was tossed around like a piece of confetti at a tickertape parade. Visibility was almost non-existent as Post sought safe ground to land. Finally he spotted a newly seeded field. Not the most artful landing he ever made—Post broke a strut in the process—but given the conditions, a near miraculous accomplishment. The experience not only solidified his standing with Hall, it convinced his boss to look for a new plane that would protect him from the elements. In 1928, Post flew to California to oversee the final touches on a Lockheed Vega, which Hall named *Winnie Mae* after his daughter. The plane was one of the first Vegas to roll out of the factory.

Post began gauging Hall's interest in letting him enter some air races and try his hand at setting a new trans-continental speed record. Before his boss could consent, the Depression hit. Hall was forced to cut his payroll and sell the *Winnie Mae* back to Lockheed, where Post secured a job as a test pilot. On a contract basis, he tried out new models, transported planes across country to customers, and worked with engineers in designing new innovations in aviation. He rubbed elbows with famous aviators like Amelia Earhart, testing a used Lockheed plane for her—she called it "third-hand clunk," he called it dangerous—and convinced the company to give her a different one.

Months later, Hall phoned to tell him times were better and offered Post his old job back. "I want a new ship," Hall said, "and I'll let you make some of those flights you were figuring on last year." He asked Post to order a Vega and make any improvements he wanted.

Wiley Post described the day it came off the assembly lines as one of the greatest of his life. It was "about the last word in airplanes," Post wrote in a letter to his wife. The new *Winnie Mae* cost $22,000 and could seat seven, with a 420-horsepower Pratt & Whitney Wasp engine. He had Lockheed set the wing at a slightly lower angle to lessen wind drag at high speeds and took four inches off the tail to prevent it from bouncing on rough landings. Additional fuel tanks increased capacity by 500 gallons. All this added 10 mph to its top speed.

With a state-of-the-art craft at his disposal, Wiley Post entered his first race in 1930, an air derby between Los Angeles and Chicago, which, with a purse of $7,500, had attracted the world's top pilots. The odds of an unknown flier from Oklahoma winning were a thousand to one. But Wiley Post had been fighting odds his whole life.

Post sought out navigator savant Harold Gatty, who Will Rogers would later say could "take a $1.00 Ingersoll watch, a Woolworth compass, and a lantern, and at twelve o'clock at night tell you just how many miles the American farmer is away from the poor house." Post and Gatty immediately hit it off. Neither was exactly sociable. They didn't drink or smoke and mumbled when thrust into the public spotlight, but never tired of talking about aviation. Gatty stayed up all night before the race and handed Post his charts and maps just before takeoff. This was Post's first attempt at flying with navigational tools; until then he had flown strictly by feel. With Gatty's charts, Post found himself pushed by a tremendous tailwind when suddenly his compass malfunctioned. He was entirely dependent on the maps for navigation.

On August 27, 1930, Post hit Chicago after averaging 192 mph. Because each racer's start was staggered, Post had to wait to see how he ranked. He was such an unknown that race officials didn't even know who he was when he checked in after landing. The next day "a plane like mine grew out of the west, took shape, and flashed across the finish line," Post said. "And what ship do you think he was flying? You bet! The old *Winnie Mae*." More dinged up and repainted, the old *Winnie Mae*, which Hall had sold back to Lockheed, had a new owner and a new pilot, Art Goebel, former holder of the transcontinental record.

Wiley Post was the winner by eleven seconds, a feat that earned him $7500 and national recognition. Even more improbable was that Harold Gatty had also counseled Goebel.

The two top fliers had flown *Winnie Mae*s and relied on the same navigator. "That clinched the slight little Australian with me," Post said later. Gatty was going to help him achieve his dream.

Like most pilots, Post abhorred the idea that the speed record for flying around the world was held by a dirigible, which he and other aviators derisively referred to as a "balloon": the Graf Zeppelin, piloted by Hugo Eckener in 1929 with a time of 21 days. Gatty "was going around the world with me, although he didn't know that at the time. I would take him if I had to shanghai him." It didn't take much convincing.

The two, communicating though a plastic tube, left New York's Roosevelt Field on June 23, 1931, stopping at Harbor Grace, Newfoundland, for refueling and then continuing over the ocean, winging into black Atlantic skies and torrential rain halfway across, with Post flying blind almost the entire time. "Don't bother me with your damn directions now," Post shouted at Gatty after one particularly hard jolt. "Wait till we get out of this soup, and then I'll be tickled to death if you can tell us where we are." When they spotted land, Gatty thought they might be nearing Ireland or maybe Scotland. It turned out to be Chester, England.

Dirty weather plagued the duo virtually their entire journey. They didn't have the benefit of reliable navigation aids or accurate maps, so they followed railroads and rivers through Europe and flew under storm clouds because they couldn't maneuver around mountains. Only rarely could Gatty rely on the sun to get their bearings.

In Russia the duo encountered thick fog and sheets of rain: "It was just as if a fire hose were being turned through that opening in front of the engine cowl," Post said. Flying blind over the ocean was stressful enough, but they could count on plenty of altitude and nothing to hit. "Hedge-hopping through Russia," however, with 200 yards' visibility at over 100 miles per hour "is enough to make your hair stand on end every time you cross a fence."

It was getting dark when Post and Gatty approached Blagoveshchensk, almost 5000 miles east of Moscow. They flew over the Amur River, but Post couldn't find the airport, which was supposed to have been marked by oil flares. After circling the city a few times, their fuel running low, Gatty spotted a string of dim lights lining the east bank of the river. As Post drew near, he thought it might be a lake, since all he could see was water. The flares cast a reflection with the sort of widening beam the moon throws on a pond. If this were the landing strip, it was going to be tricky.

"Get as far back as you can," Post told Gatty. "Hold your instruments so they won't break. Set yourself for a jolt and hang on like hell." Post tried not to sound panicked. Normally night landings didn't bother him, but when the only lights shine on water and offer only the hint at a rectangle, you're placing faith in forces far beyond one human pilot. Post was feeling decidedly unconfident.

Keeping the *Winnie Mae*'s tail down and slowing the engine to 900 rpms, Post eased the ship down. He kept his hand on the throttle just in case he needed to get away fast should the runway prove to be even rougher and more pock-marked than the other Russian runways they had experienced. Moving the stick around like a coffee stirrer, coming in at more than 100 miles an hour, he aimed his wheels for the first half-dry path he saw, missing by only a few feet.

There was no bounce when the *Winnie Mae* struck land. Mud clogged the wheel guards and water sprayed all around. Post fought the controls, desperate to keep the tail on the ground, even though he knew they were traveling much too fast over this muck. They rolled about 400 feet, the ship getting heavier and heavier. Post tried to turn the left wheel and the ship promptly sank. The two fliers jumped out into a light drizzle, slipping and sliding in two inches of water over a foot of ooze. Post searched for a rock to prop under one of the wheels to stop the plane from sinking further.

A ramshackle car splashed toward them and out stepped two Danish telegraph operators, who produced a rope. While Post gunned his engine they gunned theirs, but the car was too light and its wheels spun helplessly, kicking up black mud. After an hour of fruitless pulling, they agreed to abandon the plane and head to a nearby administration building to think things through. Conditions were even worse further down the runway.

When they entered the well-lit office, Gatty got his first good look at Post and promptly keeled over laughing. Post's clothes stuck to his skin in odd little folds and his face was painted with mud. "He wore that dejected look of comic pathos with which Charlie Chaplin established the reputation that brought him fame and fortune," Gatty later recalled. "And the muddy water from the field dripped to a pool about his indefinitely shaped feet."

Post glared at Gatty, who was also a wreck, and offered a pained grin.

Exhausted and dispirited, they shuffled to an open window and watched the rain spit down.

"Well, I don't think we'll have much trouble with the

navigation for the next few hours," Gatty said.

"No," Post replied, "and we can be roommates in the poorhouse, or maybe in the nuthouse, if we don't get out of here by morning."

Post trudged out to the plane to grab some shuteye in the cockpit, while Gatty accompanied the Danes to town for a meal. By morning the rain stopped, and the wind partially dried out the loamy black soil where the plane sat. Some Russians who worked at the airfield volunteered some horses, but as soon as they heard the engine they almost bolted. After they calmed down, Post turned up the engine again, but the horses simply could not extricate the two-ton ship from the gooey mess. Five hours later the ground had hardened enough to offer the horses a foothold, and with a dozen locals pulling on ropes and pushing on the fuselage, the *Winnie Mae* finally popped free. More than 12 hours after being stranded, they were airborne again.

Blagoveshchensk wasn't the last place they encountered trouble. Gale force winds delayed their take off for five hours in Khabarovsk, and all over Siberia they kept getting lost, due to inaccurate Russian maps. Post climbed above the clouds so Gatty could take a bearing from the sun. They flew hundreds of extra miles just to get back on track. By the time they hit the beach at Solomon, Alaska, the fuel gauge was flirting with empty.

Back on American soil, they hoped their problems were over. They weren't. After purchasing fuel from a nearby store, Post almost flipped over the plane on takeoff when the *Winnie Mae*'s wheels got mired in yet more mud. The ship stood up on its nose and the propeller tips bent. After Post straightened them with a rock and a hammer, Gatty was nearly cut in half by the propeller.

En route to Fairbanks, they were accosted by more fog and hail. Waiting for them was Alaskan bush pilot Joe Crosson. Although Post and Crosson had met just two years earlier, they had become fast friends, sharing a love of hunting, fishing, and flying. Crosson had the *Winnie Mae* rolled into a hangar, and a crew of Alaskan Airways mechanics replaced the propeller and effected other repairs while Post and Gatty grabbed three hours of sleep. This wouldn't be the last time that Crosson would save Post from desperate circumstances.

More rain and mud greeted them in Edmonton, prompting Post to say he wished the *Winnie Mae* had been mounted on floats. A Canadian mail pilot suggested they take off from Portage Avenue, a cleanly paved road that ran two miles from the airfield to town. The mayor put emergency crews to work taking down the electric light wires strung alongside the road. When Post revved the motor, mud splattered those standing nearest to the *Winnie Mae*. They sped down the road, electric light poles mere inches away from the ends of their wings. Post floored it and the plane jumped to 75 mph and then lifted off the ground. It was an awesome display of piloting skill. When they flew over the Hotel MacDonald, where they had stayed, a platoon of bellhops stood on the roof and offered a salute.

In many ways, Post's visual handicap helped him because he was accustomed to flying by feel and making calculations in his head while in the air, to compensate for his lack of depth perception. He often joked that he would have to give up flying if they ever changed the height of two-story buildings.

Eight days after starting, the pair landed in New York, and the world was suddenly smaller than it ever had been. Post and Gatty received a hero's welcome—a near riot at the airport, press conferences, a tickertape parade, medals awarded by the City of New York, and a visit to the White House to meet the President. Then came a cross-country promotional tour, financed by an oil company, where the local press covered their every move.

Meanwhile, other pilots set out to best their record, just like rivals had tried to do after Lindbergh crossed the Atlantic four years earlier. Most failed; some died. Even in failure, though, some became more famous than if they had actually succeeded.

Departing soon after Post and Gatty had returned, Americans Clyde Edward "Upside Down" Pangborn and Hugh Herndon, Jr. aimed to cut two days from Post and Gatty's around-the-world record. Instead, they encountered bad weather and worse luck. After getting lost in Mongolia, they landed in the Siberian city of Khabarovsk in a torrential rainstorm, their plane sitting in the mud of the runway. By the time the storm ended, they were 27 hours behind Post and Gatty's time, which prompted them to change plans. Their new goal was to collect the $25,000 prize offered by the Japanese newspaper *Asahi Shimbun* for the first nonstop flight from Japan to the United States.

They departed for Tokyo. When they landed, they were arrested. After heavy diplomatic wrangling, they were eventually fined and released. Japanese officials warned the two pilots they would be entitled to only one take-off attempt. If they failed, or mechanical difficulty forced them down in Japanese airspace, their plane would be impounded.

It was a long shot. Their plane, the *Bellanca*, would be overloaded with 930 gallons of fuel and weigh 9000 pounds, far more than the manufacturer advised. To even the odds, they devised a mechanism to jettison the landing gear once they were airborne, which they calculated would add 15 mph to their speed and 600 miles to their range. Three hours into the flight, the landing gear struts did not release, so Pangborn, a virtuoso wing walker, crawled outside 14,000 feet above the Pacific in freezing cold and 100-mile per hour wind and loosened the remaining struts. Forty hours later they performed a belly flop, landing on a gravel runway in Wenatchee, Washington, on October 5th, 1931, completing the first non-stop Trans-Pacific flight—and beating out Wiley Post for the Aviation League's Harmon Trophy, symbolizing the greatest achievement in flight for 1931. With Wiley Post, even when he won, he lost.

F.C. Hall, the Oklahoman oilman who had bankrolled Post and Gatty's expedition, predicted that Post would become a rich man if he succeeded in girdling the globe, estimating that the flight alone could bring in $75,000, endorsements roughly $125,000, and barnstorming tours an additional $100,000—an eye-popping amount of money in 1931. But the Depression was in full swing, and this was one bet Hall lost. The public relations firm Bruno and Blythe organized the speaking tour, which was sponsored by Mobil and the National Broadcasting Corporation (NBC). From July 18 to September 7, Post and Gatty flew to 25 cities across the country, making appearances, giving speeches and answering questions from the local press. Neither was known for the gift of gab.

One disappointed columnist for the *Oregon Daily Journal*

wrote: "Wiley Post and Harold Gatty may be a streak in the air but on the ground they're just a couple of tired-looking airmen who are record-breakers neither for talk nor action." According to the writer, when Post climbed out of the *Winnie Mae's* cockpit, he remarked he was "a little bit stiff." What pearls of wisdom did Post impart on the 50 or so people—mostly airport employees—who met him? "Ah'm hungry and ah'm goin' uptown and eat," Post drawled. Asked about his future plans, Post said he expected to finish his nation-wide tour in about ten days at New Orleans. "Then ah'm goin' to take a vacation." Gatty didn't even have that much to say. A reporter reminded him about one of his most famous students—Mrs. Charles A. Lindbergh. "She's turned out to have been a pretty good student, don't you think?" He only nodded.

The nationwide tour had been expected to bring in $20,000, but fell far short. Many cities simply didn't pay up, due to the hard times. Post and Gatty had been guaranteed $15,000, far more than the speaking engagements yielded: only $6,091.98. Post earned another $6,856.25 from the exclusive columns he sold to The *New York Times,* which were run over the transom. "The papers are just simply not buying anything in the way of features than they absolutely need," explained an enclosed note, "and even the editors who thought the flight was a brilliant achievement refused to purchase the byline story." And the ghostwritten book *Around the World in Eight Days*, which detailed Post and Gatty's historic flight, was far from a bestseller.

Then Post and Hall squabbled over Post's insistence on using the plane for personal appearances. This prompted Post to demand that Hall sell it to him. Hall drew up a bill of sale dated July 8 on hotel notepaper. Post gave him $3,000 in cash and a promissory note for $18,200, and on September 15 paid the entire balance. The *Winnie Mae* was his, although it took almost every penny he had.

After the hubbub of his adventure died down, he once again scrambled to earn a living. He thought of starting a flight school but couldn't find financial backers. Even with his accomplishments, he found it difficult to compete for flying jobs because people found it hard to trust a one-eyed pilot. Post briefly considered flying the Pacific, but Pangborn had beat him to it. With the economy reeling, only Lindbergh, who reaped millions, and Amelia Earhart were thriving, and both had enormous advantages. Lindbergh had been first, which assured that he would remain forever a household name. When Earhart wasn't lecturing for a fee, she designed her own line of clothing, wrote books—did whatever it took to keep the money rolling in, while her husband worked as her full-time publicist.

Post didn't have Lindbergh's movie star looks or Earhart's charm and poise, either. He was a country boy whose rough-hewn manners and cotton-mouthed drawl contributed to his being chronically underestimated. It led some newspapermen to suggest that Gatty the navigator was the true brains, while all Post did was sit up front and steer. Meanwhile, F.C. Hall, perhaps out of spite, bought a new Vega he christened *The Winnie Mae of Oklahoma* and hired pilot Frank Hoover, whom he planned to bankroll in a round-the-world flight. (It never got off the ground.) By winter Post was downright morose. He sat on the edge of a bed in a Chicago hotel room and told a reporter for the North American Newspaper Alliance, "Our flight didn't prove a thing. No stunt flying does. It is silly to say that such flights are made to develop aviation."

The reporter asked if Post would retire. He scoffed. "That's a good one! Lindbergh is the only guy who made enough off his flight to retire. The day of money-making flights is past. Lindbergh was the one and only 'natural.' A man who knows was telling me how much that fellow made. It is unbelievable; the public has no idea. It's partly the hard times, of course, that killed the game. But the public seems to have lost interest as well."

If retirement was out, what did Post plan to do? "Oh, I suppose I'll stick to aviation," he said. "I've had some offers."

As 1931 came to a merciful end, Post had managed to keep the *Winnie Mae* in the air. That in and of itself was an accomplishment. But the economy in 1932 further deteriorated, and he couldn't cover the cost of fuel. Between September 15, 1931 and March 15, 1932, Post logged 400 hours in the sky; from March 15 to September 15, he flew just 14 hours. He wasn't the only struggling airman. That year there would be only five trans-Atlantic flights attempts, with Jimmie Mattern and Bennett Griffin piloting one of them. Even if Post could somehow scrounge up the resources to puddle-hop the Atlantic, he knew it wouldn't be nearly enough in the eyes of the public.

An even more ambitious plan began to take shape.

CHAPTER 4

Gliders, Balloons, and the Vega

FOR MORE THAN THREE CENTURIES, SAILING SHIPS HELD a monopoly on trans-global travel—from the time Magellan's ship limped home (without him) after three and a half years at sea until steamers shaved the time to span oceans to months and railways connected towns and cities across contiguous continents. This prompted Jules Verne to write of a fictitious round-the-world trip by the equally fictitious Phileas Fogg, who circled the globe in 80 days by ship, train, and even elephant. Verne's classic was the inspiration for famed journalist Nellie Bly, who bested Fogg by eight days in 1872 on a trip her newspaper sponsored. Three decades later, faster steamships and railroads, with more routes and hubs, and the advent of the automobile, made a globe-gallivanting expedition possible in less than half the time: In 1913, John H. Mears accomplished it in 35 days, 21 hours, and 36 minutes.

Then came World War I and the emergence of air travel, which whittled down the record more. In 1926, Edward S. Evans and Linton Wells logged 18,000 miles in 28 days, 14 hours, 36 minutes, and 5 seconds riding in 12 airplanes, an automobile, several ships, and an array of small boats and other land vehicles. They would have made better time if they had been able to soar over oceans, like Lindbergh, who crossed the Atlantic in *The Spirit of St. Louis* the following year, ushering in the age of aerial conquest.

Suddenly there was a mad dash to set new speed and distance records—the first to cross the Atlantic the other way (from Europe to the U.S.), traverse the Pacific, go from Europe to Australia, scale the North and South Poles, make it to Ireland from America, fly cross country from New York to California without stopping to refuel. Only a blimp, the Zeppelin, had circumnavigated the entire world by air, taking 21 days. That was until Wiley Post and Harold Gatty did it in eight days in 1931. *The New York Times* headlines from that day sums up the intense enthusiasm the public received the news:

POST AND GATTY GET STIRRING WELCOME

CROWDS CHEER WORLD FLIERS IN PARADE

WALKER DECORATES THEM AT CITY HALL
CONFETTI STORM IS BIGGEST

THOUSANDS LINED BROADWAY TO GIVE A RECEPTION LIKE THAT TO LINDBERGH

Naturally it was the advent of mechanical, heavier-than-air flight that made this possible—something that had intrigued humans since our ancestors first started cooking with fire and etching art on cave walls. On the walls of the Lascaux caves in central France is a painting of an inscrutable birdman that dates back 16,000 years. In Greek mythology, more than a thousand years before the birth of Christ, there was the story of Icarus, whose father, a master craftsman, forged wings for his son from feathers and wax. Icarus brushed off parental warnings about flying too close to the sun, and, his enthusiasm getting the best of him, tried out a series of gravity-defying tricks that pushed him higher and higher until the wax melted, the feathers came loose, and he plummeted to his death.

Over the next 2000 years, inventors in China and Europe experimented with kites, balloons, and primitive gliders, almost always modeled on birds; but there are no reliable accounts of humans taking flight until the year 1000, when the English Benedictine monk Eilmer of Malmesbury fashioned a glider and traveled 600 feet through the air before crashing and badly injuring himself. Six centuries hence, Leonardo da Vinci imagined his own hang glider, which he wisely never took out for a spin.

Given gliders' obvious and inherent dangers, it's not surprising that humans' first extended air travel occurred in balloons. What is surprising is who managed it first: two bumbling French brothers who, without understanding basic science, based their work on bizarre theories and mumbo jumbo.

On June 4, 1783, at the marketplace in Annonay, France, six years before the onset of the French Revolution, Joseph-Michel and Jacques-Étienne Montgolfier, sons of a wealthy paper manufacturer, invited nobles and peasants alike to the main square of their hometown to gather around their giant globe-shaped balloon. Stitched from four humongous sections of sackcloth with three layers of thin paper forming an inner chamber and held together with 1800 buttons, the balloon was 66 feet in diameter, engorged with 28,000 cubic feet of hot, smoky air, and weighed 500 pounds.

The 12th of 16 children, Joseph, born in 1740, had always been the maverick of the family. After running away from school as a teenager, he picked mulberry leaves before going into business for himself selling chemical products. Slovenly in dress and manner, he spent his meager wages on mathematics and physics textbooks. While his father eventually convinced him to enter the family business, he spent most of his time daydreaming. In contrast, the younger Jacques-Étienne, born in 1745, was diligent, sociable, and very smart—his nickname was the "calculating machine"—the public face of the family who was good with business and comfortable mixing with the elite and hoi polloi alike. He studied architecture in Paris where he hobnobbed with great scientists of his time such as Benjamin Franklin.

It was Joseph, however, who had first conceived of balloon travel six years earlier. Depending on which version of his story you believe—he was an unreliable narrator—the epiphany struck him when he watched his wife's chemise lift off when placed before a fire to dry; or maybe it was his own shirt, although it didn't lift off, he simply noticed it was billowing, with pockets of air pushing it up. Then again, it could have been a loaf wrapping his wife tossed on the flames, which, when it began to burn, rose into the air; or perhaps it was after Joseph read up on British scientist Dr. Joseph Priestly's experiments with different types of air.

Joseph didn't get around to conducting any experiments of his own until November 1792. One day, as he watched flames lick the air, his mind wandered, as it was wont to do, and he thought about the best way to attack a well-protected fortress like Gibraltar, which was considered impregnable by both land and sea. What if, he wondered, soldiers could be transported into the air by the same force that lifted the embers in a fire? He decided that within the heated air, there must be a gas—he dubbed it "Montgolfier Gas"—that was visible as smoke and possessed special properties he attributed to "levity." Of course, he was completely wrong about that: Hot air rises because the air expands when it's heated, so that its weight is reduced as volume increases. On the basis of who knows what, he concluded the best gas would come from burning a mix of chopped wool and damp straw. Later, he and his brother would throw old boots and rotting meat into the fires, believing these raised the fuel's octane.

To test his theories Joseph constructed an envelope out of taffeta (a crisp, smooth woven fabric made from silk) ribbed with an internal frame of very light wood and designed with an open neck at the bottom. He wadded up and then lit some paper, filling the envelope with hot air and smoke, watching in amazement as his creation rose to the ceiling. Joseph immediately wrote his brother: "Prepare supplies of taffeta and rope and you will see one of the most astounding things in the world!" Outside he repeated the experiment for his brother, and the balloon soared 60 feet into the air. He told his brother those British soldiers that protected Gibraltar from French and Spanish troops wouldn't stand a chance.

The two erstwhile inventors pooled their resources for a development program to build and test successfully larger balloons. In December 1782, they constructed what they called an aerostat, three times bigger and 27 times larger in air volume than the prototype Joseph had tried out in his room. On its maiden voyage it took off so fast they lost control and the balloon soared more than a mile from where it took off. Eventually it was destroyed through the "indiscretion" of passersby, no doubt alarmed by the strange object that had fallen from the sky. The following April they tested a balloon 30 feet in diameter, which achieved an altitude of 600 feet and floated with the wind for more than half a mile.

To stake a claim to their invention, the brothers needed witnesses, and invited practically the whole town to come watch their next test flight. In front of an audience of hundreds, the Montgolfiers had their helpers inflate their latest and greatest vessel, which at 28,000 cubic feet was more than twice the size of the one they had tested two months earlier. When released, the balloon climbed to more than 3000 feet and covered a mile and a half in the ten minutes it remained aloft, coming down gradually as the air inside cooled. Man had finally defied gravity and created a machine that could fly. Word quickly spread to Paris.

The French Academy of Sciences received with disdain the news of the brothers' exploits, miffed that two ignorant non-scientists had created the first flying ship. This would not do; hence the academy supported the quest of one of its members, a young physicist named Jacques Alexandre César Charles, who immediately attempted to reproduce the Montgolfiers' experiments. Along the way, Charles noted that the volume of a gas is directly proportional to its temperature, a phenomenon he called Charles Law, which is still used to this day.

Professor Charles suggested a hydrogen-filled balloon made from a silk envelope and coated with a rubber solution to make it leak-proof, which scientific research indicated should fly higher and faster than any hot air balloon. It took him a little more than two months to construct the balloon and four days to mix the hydrogen, which required him to douse 1000 pounds of iron filings with 500 pounds of sulfuric acid—at the time, the largest quantity of hydrogen ever produced.

On a rainy late August day, Charles waited for a cannon shot before untethering the 12-foot tall aerostat from Champ de Mars in Paris, where, it was said, half the population came to watch, only those with tickets allowed anywhere near. It shot 3000 feet into the atmosphere in just minutes, and when it disappeared from sight, another cannon shot was fired to bid it *adieu*. Three-quarters of an hour later it alighted 18 miles away in a field in the village of Gonesse, where peasants thought it might be a giant bird or invaders from the moon and tore it to bits with pitchforks and scythes. For good measure they strapped the fabric to a horse's tail and sent him galloping through the field, until there was hardly a trace of Charles' balloon.

Meanwhile, Jacques-Étienne Montgolfier was also in Paris to arrange a public demonstration, securing the support of King Louis XVI and funding from the government,

as well as finessing a joint venture with wallpaper manufacturer Jean-Baptiste Réveillon, which provided the paper for
the brothers' next balloon. It was their biggest yet: 66 feet
tall, 40-plus feet wide, fueled with 50 pounds of damp straw
and wool, and the exterior decorated in 18th century sky blue
wallpaper with accents of gold, signs of the zodiac, and suns.
Things went as planned until a sudden storm broke, the
wallpaper dissolved, and the vessel flopped to the ground a
sodden mess.

Undeterred, the Montgolfiers got to work on a replace-
ment comprised of taffeta coated with aluminum varnish
that had fire-prevention properties, and decided to include
the first air passengers—not people, since no one knew what
effect high altitudes would have on humans, but animals.
After mulling over a horse or an ox, they opted for a duck,
a rooster, and a sheep they named Montauciel ("Climb-to-
the-sky"). They figured winged animals should have little
problem with altitude, while conventional wisdom of their
day held that sheep most closely approximated the physi-
ology of humans. (Use your imagination to figure out they
came up with that.)

King Louis XVI and Marie Antoinette attended the next
launch of a *montgolfière*, which commenced from the front
courtyard of Château de la Muette, the king's estate near the
house of Réveillon. A wicker basket containing the caged
livestock was attached to the bottom, and adding to the
poundage of straw and wool fuel were some old boots and
rotting meat, which the brothers believed would increase the
autostat's lift. At one p.m., after lunch with the monarch,
the brothers released the balloon from a special fire platform
to the cheers of the crowd. One intrigued onlooker was fel-

low scientist and envoy to France from the United States Benjamin Franklin. When asked of what use the balloon would be, he famously retorted, "What use, sir, is a newborn baby?"

Toting its animal carriage, the balloon traveled two miles, landing gently enough in the Vaucresson Forest. The first on the scene, arriving on horseback, was 30-year-old scientist Jean-François Pilâtre de Rozier, head of the king's natural history collection. He rooted around for the livestock, which were buried under the balloon's deflated skin. When he opened the cage he discovered the duck and sheep dazed but unscathed, though the rooster had injured one of its wings, which could have happened any time during the flight and for any number of reasons.

Back at the royal estate, King Louis expressed his delight with the results of this grand experiment by ordering the animals cooked for dinner. Then Jacques-Étienne Montgolfier informed his majesty, well known for his indecisiveness, that the next balloon should carry a man, a suggestion that de Rozier seconded.

Absolutely not, Louis replied. He might have pointed out that theologians were dead set against the idea. God would not approve of ballooning, and any man who went up in *one* would be approaching the gates of Heaven before his proper time. Or perhaps it was his mood.

Nevertheless, Montgolfier and de Rozier persisted.

Very well, his highness said, provided the flying men were condemned criminals, whom he would pardon if they survived, which he thought unlikely.

De Rozier protested, arguing that the glory of the first flight should not be given to criminals. He enlisted the aid of François Laurent, who was the Marquis d'Arlandes and a cousin of the king. D'Arlandes in turn petitioned Marie Antoinette to convince Louis to change his royal mind, which he did. Unfortunately for de Rozier, d'Arlandes now insisted on joining him on the maiden voyage.

As autumn merged with winter, de Rozier and the Montgolfier brothers worked on a larger, more durable vessel that looked like a humongous lemon, equipped with a circular wicker compartment in the shape of a bracelet and hung near the bottom with a separate iron fire basket. The balloon's skin was painted blue and gold and ornamented with gold *fleurs-de-lis*, the monogram of Louis XVI.

No one thought it prudent to dispatch two men into the atmosphere without first conducting tests. The group settled on ropes to hold the balloon in place while de Rozier climbed aboard and was slowly raised to a height of 80 feet, where he maintained his position by fine-tuning the fire's intensity. Four days later, de Rozier rose to 250 feet, the vessel was pulled down, the Marquis d'Arlandes joined him onboard, and the two floated up to 350 feet.

On the appointed hour and day, November 21, 1783, at Château de la Muette, the sky was partly cloudy and the wind puffed in from the northwest. The first attempt at taking off went awry, however, when a hard gust blew the balloon into one of the garden walks. The ropes rubbed against the fabric, causing several tears, the longest stretching six feet. Two hours later at 1:54 p.m., after repairs were affected, the world's first aeronauts set off. There was a hush as the balloon cut a majestic figure as it rose over the palace. "No one could help feeling a mingled sentiment of fear and admiration," attested an octet of observers that again included

Benjamin Franklin in a signed affidavit later that day.

Adrift in the wind 270 feet up, the balloon passed a hedge and did a half turn. Onboard, d'Arlandes was astonished by the crowd's unexpected quiescence. Perhaps they are frightened, he reasoned. He waved but there was no discernible response, so he shook his handkerchief and "immediately perceived a great movement in the garden," he wrote in a letter dated a week later. "It seemed as if the spectators all formed one mass, which rushed, by an involuntary motion, towards the wall, which it seemed to consider as the only obstacle between us."

His partner in flight interrupted his reverie, one nobleman to another: "You are doing nothing," de Rozier remarked, "and the balloon is scarcely rising a fathom."

D'Arlandes begged his pardon, stirred the fire, and then tossed in a brick of straw. Ascending quickly, he was having trouble getting a fix on their position. They were so high he could not make out individual buildings, not even the Château de la Muette from whence they had begun their journey. Following the serpentine path of the Seine until he could identify the bends in the river, and recognizing the Visitation de Chaillot, a mammoth double-winged palace on the bank of the river, he ticked off each neighborhood. "Passy, St. Germain, St. Denis, Sèvres!"

"If you look at the river in that fashion you will be likely to bathe in it soon," de Rozier, ever the taskmaster, cried. "Some fire, my dear friend. Some fire."

Left to the wind's whims, their craft appeared reluctant to cross the river and instead hovered over the water and headed upstream. Neither welcomed this turn of events; they would have preferred to hover over terra firma in case they needed to land. Some minutes later, d'Arlandes said, "Here is a river which is very difficult to cross."

"So it seems," de Rozier replied, "but you are doing nothing. I suppose it is because you are braver than I, and don't fear a tumble."

D'Arlandes poked the fire and seized a truss of straw with his fork, which being pressed too tightly, wouldn't light. He shook it over the flames and a tremendous heat seized his armpits. "We are rising now," he called.

Suddenly d'Arlandes heard a loud noise originate from the top of the balloon, so loud and forceful he thought it might have popped. When he looked, however, he saw nothing out of sorts. De Rozier climbed above to investigate. Without warning they were jolted straight up. "What are you doing up there—dancing?" d'Arlandes asked.

"I am not stirring," de Rozier said.

"So much the better," d'Arlandes said. "This must be a new current, which will, I hope, take us off the river."

It did. They drifted over the city to surrounding countryside.

D'Arlandes heard a new noise, and investigating, discovered a plethora of flaming holes, some alarmingly large, breaking out on the south side of the balloon. "We must get down!" d'Arlandes shouted.

"Why?" de Rozier asked.

"Look!" D'Arlandes grabbed a sponge to extinguish the flames closest to him. "We must descend!"

De Rozier surveyed the landscape and pointed out they were over Paris.

D'Arlandes tested the cords connecting the fire iron to the balloon. Two had snapped, but the rest seemed sound.

He suggested they cross the city to locate a suitable place to land. They were like passengers on an out-of-control coach over rough roads, speeding toward a patch of roofs. If they ran into them, they would either die from the impact or from the inevitable flames that would consume them. They reignited the fire by throwing more bricks of straw and wool into the embers, and their craft responded by arcing over the top.

As they sped downhill, the wind shifted and pushed them south toward the heavily wooded Luxembourg Gardens. De Rozier artfully fine-tuned their final descent by feeding small portions of straw and wool to the fire to slow their descent. They sped over a major boulevard—the last major obstacle before open plains beckoned—and de Rozier completely suppressed the fire. The balloon got smaller and smaller as they headed lower and lower.

Finally, 25 minutes after they had departed, near a mill in Butte-aux-Cailles, a neighborhood located on hills in the southeast corner of the city, they hit the ground with a jolt. D'Arlandes felt balloon fabric plop down softly on his head. He pushed it off and leaped out. Turning towards the balloon, he noted to his astonishment that it was perfectly empty and flattened, like a soufflé that had collapsed in the oven.

De Rozier crept from under the sea of canvas that had draped over him, in shirtsleeves because he had used his coat to tamp down the many fires that had plagued their flight. Since it was cold, the two aero-voyagers set out for the nearest house to seek warmth, anointed national heroes of France.

Two weeks later, on December 1, 1783, a mammoth

crowd 400,000 people—at the time the city's population was barely 600,000—gathered in the vicinity of the Jardin des Tuileries in Paris to witness the young physicist from the French Academy of Science, Jacques Charles, pilot a hydrogen balloon with Nicholas-Louis Robert. Rising to 1800 feet, they sailed 20 miles in two hours and five minutes, coming down in Nesles-la-Vallée as the sun was setting. Robert got out and Charles flew solo, climbing rapidly to 9000 feet, where he became the first man to greet both a sunset and sunrise in a balloon. After experiencing crushing pain in his ears, however, he promptly descended and never flew again.

Then in Lyon on January 19, 1784, 100,000 spectators congregated to witness the dispatch of another *montgolfière*, their biggest yet, which was sponsored by the governor of Lyon. This time six men were on board, including de Rozier and its inventor Joseph Montgolfier. In true madcap fashion, there was a scuffle as the balloon was launched when a seventh man, Claudius Fontaine, jumped into the basket. He had assisted Joseph with the initial experiments and often begged to be the first to fly, having missed out when the honor had been bestowed on de Rozier.

To make up for this slight, Joseph promised he could come with him. On the blessed day, however, Prince Charles-Joseph Lamoral de Ligne informed Fontaine there was no room. The balloon was at a considerable height before anyone other than Joseph noticed the stowaway. The Prince of Ligne was angry, but Fontaine cut him off, saying, "Princes may consider themselves our superiors on earth, but in the aerial regions we are now exploring, we are all equal, and on the same level." The trip was truncated when at 3000 feet a large section of fabric ripped. The balloon hurtled to earth, landing roughly and leaving the men shaken but otherwise unharmed.

This would be the Montgolfiers' last balloon. After King Louis XVI elevated their father to the nobility and honored them with crest that read SIC ITURE AD ASTRA (*Thus we go to the stars*), Joseph and Jacques-Étienne returned to papermaking, their inheritance largely spent. The balloon, Jacques-Étienne wrote in a letter later that year, "is a beautiful fruit, but it is not ripe. We will be dead before the sun of practice and experience will ripen it. It is a tree we have planted for our nephews."

While he and his brother were the first to send men into the sky, it was the hydrogen balloon that became all the rage in 18th century Europe, validating Charles' vision. These early flights were a sensation, drawing millions of people across Europe to bear witness to history. Coins were minted and engravings etched to commemorate them. Shopkeepers sold enamel and gilt-bronze replicas, crockery and clocks with balloon-shaped dials, jewelry, lanterns in the shape of *montgolfières*, paintings, and balloon-back chairs.

As for de Rozier, he requested 40,000 francs from the crown the following year to build a balloon to bring glory to France as first to cross the English Channel. It was, he argued, a matter of national pride. Slender as a French coin and utterly fearless, de Rozier designed his balloon to be a cross between a *montgolfière* and Charles' hydrogen version: The lower part was pumped with hot air while the upper section was a huge hydrogen bubble. De Rozier reasoned that "when I wish to descend I shall simply cool the hot air in the *montgolfières* instead of letting out the gas. Then, to rise again it would only be necessary to rekindle the fire. This also renders ballast unnecessary." Logical on some levels, perhaps, but Professor Charles called it for what it was: "like lighting a fire under a barrel of gunpowder."

De Rozier transported his balloon to the coastal city of Boulogne and waited, the wind cold, unforgiving, and—worst of all—blowing from England to France. At the same time, Englishman Jean-Pierre Blanchard and American actor John Jeffries were in Dover preparing to cross from the other side. Each day de Rozier waited for the wind to change, and each day he returned to his inn disappointed. He dispatched trial balloons in the hopes they might rise into a crosscurrent, but they all returned to France.

On January 7, 1785, Blanchard and Jeffries took off from southern England. Partway across, the balloon lost gas and they started sinking toward the gray, choppy waters of the Channel. Frantically they threw overboard everything they could think of—all of their ballast and most of their clothing—and somehow managed to remain aloft. The only cargo they kept was the first international airmail, which they delivered upon landing in Felmore Forest, France. They completed their 28-mile journey in about two and a half hours.

Always the gentleman, de Rozier was one of the first to congratulate his rivals. He might have been satisfied to seek other challenges, but the King's men reminded him that he could still fly across the Channel the other way; that way France could still have its glory. At any rate, it would not look good if de Rozier wasted 40,000 francs.

He returned to his balloon, which by this point was weather-beaten, the taffeta chewed up by packs of rats. At seven a.m. on June 15th, de Rozier and his friend, a doctor named Pierre Romain, reluctantly set sail for England. They floated out over the surf until the wind returned, urging them back to France. For the next half hour their hybrid fire and gas balloon was stuck in time and space, 1000 feet above the shore. Suddenly de Rozier made what witnesses described as a gesture of alarm, and a blue flame leaped from the bottom of the balloon. There was an explosion, and the two men hurtled to their deaths. Thus de Rozier was not only the first man to fly in a balloon, but had the dubious distinction of being the first killed in one, too.

Despite the dangers, ballooning became a popular pastime. Balloons saw action in war, first in France at the end of the 18th century, and then during America's Civil War, where they were used for mapping territory and enemy reconnaissance. In 1852 Henri Gifford invented a steerable balloon powered by a steam engine, but it wasn't until Santos-Dumont, the Brazilian heir of a coffee producer, designed a blimp equipped with an internal combustion engine and propeller that they became (somewhat) practical.

An eccentric and self-professed "sportsman of the air," the 5'4" Santos-Dumont built almost a dozen dirigibles he flew around Paris as others would drive horse-drawn carriages. He parked his blimp in front of his Champs-Élysées apartment, tied to a gas lamppost, and flew to Maxim's for dinner. During the day he took his blimp out for a leisurely spin, went shopping, or dropped in on friends, often floating down in front of a fashionable café for lunch. He might have also been the first civilian to wear a wristwatch after asking a friend, Louis Cartier, to design a timepiece he could wear while flying. (Until then only soldiers wore watches.) At the turn of the 20th century, he achieved fame for piloting his motorized dirigible around the Eiffel Tour, winning a prize, which he donated to charity.

Meanwhile, across the Atlantic, two Americans were on the verge of making history with a machine that would leave dirigibles in the dust and ultimately spawn the Golden Age of Aviation.

CHAPTER 5

Upon the Wings of Two Men

W ILBUR WRIGHT, A BICYCLE SHOP OWNER AND mechanic from Dayton, Ohio, dashed off a letter, dated May 30, 1899, to the Smithsonian Institute. He confessed that he had been interested in "the problem of mechanical and human flight since I was a boy," and that his "observations since have only convinced me more firmly that human flight is possible and practicable. It is only a question of knowledge and skill just as in all acrobatic feats." He explained that he intended to conduct a systematic study. "I am an enthusiast," he added, "but not a crank in the sense that I have some pet theories as to the proper construction of a flying machine," and requested any papers or research the Institute could send.

Wilbur Wright, then in his early 30s and unmarried, was lean, bald, and bird-like, with thin lips and gray-blue eyes. His father was a minister and he hailed from a family of modest mid-western means. As a teenager he was an excellent student and fine athlete, skillful at figure skating, gymnastics, particularly the horizontal bar, and hockey. His family moved to Dayton and he never finished high school, and throughout his twenties he was sickly, afflicted with a serious type of chronic fatigue syndrome that was never fully diagnosed or understood. As biographer James Tobin wrote, he "spent most of his twenties, the age when most people find their place in life, not at all sure he would live to see his thirties."

The young Wilbur took responsibility for the care of his mother, who had been stricken with tuberculosis, and the two rarely left the house. He kept his mind active by helping his father with church business and embarking on a rigorous course of self-study. The family's bookshelves were crammed with classic literature, Greek and Roman philosophy, European history, full sets of the Encyclopedia Britannica and Chambers Cyclopedia, treatises on mathematics and science, and Wilbur was blessed with such a good memory that two decades years later, while traveling in Europe, he could recite precise details of a battle fought in a particular village in Napoleon's time.

His brother, Orville, four years his junior, also displayed preternatural talents. At 17, after spending two years as a printer's apprentice, he built a printing press from spare parts and scrap that included a buggy, a tombstone, and firewood, which could print a thousand pages an hour. Like his older brother, he dropped out of school before his senior year, and the two used Orville's printing press to start a business and publish two short-lived newspapers. Then came the bicycle boom of the gay old 1890s. Orville bought a bike in 1892 and began racing. Leery of taxing his health, Will, as his friends and family called him, was content to take long rides in the countryside. Eventually the brothers became bored with the printing business and opened a bicycle repair shop.

In 1894, they came across an article titled "The Flying Man" in *McClure's* magazine, a profile on German engineer Otto Lilienthal, who had devoted the better part of two decades to studying birds to inform his construction of gliders. After extensive trial-and-error with flat wings and hard, rigid surfaces, Lilienthal theorized that the wing's gentle parabolic curve gave birds the ability to fly, even to soar, without the need to exert energy. The rising, circling patterns of a carrier pigeon depended on this principle: He flies with the wind, but soars against it. The fins of many fish and webbed feet of aquatic birds were similarly constructed. Lilienthal reasoned that a sail wouldn't work if it were a hard, flat surface. It is the effort of the sail to get away from the wind it gathers that pushes the boat forward.

At the time, conventional wisdom, buttressed by numerous academic and scientific bodies, claimed it was impossible for man to fly, since it violated the tenets of basic physics. Therefore, since the days of Montgolfier a hundred years earlier, ballooning had received most of the attention to the detriment of human flying. "I have always regarded the balloon, and the exclusive attention which it so long attracted, as a hindrance rather than a help to the development of the art of flight," Lilienthal told *McClure's*. "If it had never been invented, it is probable that more serious investigations would have been prosecuted towards other solutions of the problem." Ballooning, he pointed out, has nothing to do with the birds, which he believed must form the model for human flight. "What we are seeking is the means of free motion in the air, in any direction. In this the balloon is of no aid; there is no relation between the two systems."

With gliders crafted from tightly woven muslin stretched over split willow branches, Lilienthal, who built his own artificial hill outside of Berlin, traveled hundreds of feet, "sailing"—his preferred term—thousands of times by controlling his direction though the manipulation of his lower body. He became so proficient that he could parry a ten-mile-an-hour updraft against a hill to hang in the air, perfectly still, while simultaneously directing a photographer into position for the perfect shot.

During the two years following the article's publication, Lilienthal began work on a glider powered by an engine he designed himself. He would never complete it. On August 9, 1896, while on a routine dash through the air, his glider suddenly lost altitude. He fell 50 feet, fracturing his spine. The next day, just before dying in a Berlin hospital, he reputedly said, "Small sacrifices must be made."

While the *McClure's* article made a lasting impression, it was Lilienthal's death, Wilbur Wright remarked later, that prompted him to pull a book on animal mechanism from the family bookshelf that he had previously read several times. He thought it likely that Lilienthal had crashed from being unable to control his glider. Lilienthal had shown the possibility of propelling a man into the air. But, Wright figured, the ability to stop was perhaps even more important than accelerating. Indeed, it wasn't until George Westinghouse invented the air brake in 1868, after all, that trains could run faster and pull hundreds of cars. Before that train wrecks were common even as trains crawled across the land. Bicycles, a subject he knew well, didn't become popular until they were equipped with a way to safely come to a complete halt either. What's more, nature had granted birds a means to balance and control their flight, which, he figured, could inform humans; but he didn't find answers in the book.

Meanwhile, others attempted to succeed where Lilienthal had failed. Later that year Samuel Langley fired a motorized glider off a floating platform that stayed in the air for one minute and 45 seconds, covering almost a mile. In 1897 British inventor Percy Pilcher, a disciple of Lilienthal's, set a record for non-motorized flight in a glider, cruising 750 feet, and Augustus Herring strapped a compressed air motor to a glider designed by Octave Chanute, managing to hop up and down a Michigan beach.

Wilbur Wright shared his ideas with his brother Orville, and at some point Wilbur's growing interest in flying, about which he had used words like *I, me,* and *my* in his Smithsonian letter, transitioned to *we, us,* and *our*. Seeking a way to control flight became their obsession, and along the way the Wrights became the ultimate do-it-yourselfers, funding their interest in flying with money they made operating their bike store.

The brothers pored over texts on ornithology and entomology and debated how one actually balances on a bicycle (notably a skill humans could learn and never forgot), wondering if it could be applied to gliding. They spent hours observing birds, wondering if they flew by shifting body weight, as Lilienthal had proposed, or by somehow manipulating their wings. From a pigeon's rapid movements that were far too speedy to be from shifting body weight, Wilbur decided that the wings, through subtle movements, must provide aerodynamic control, but it depended on the bird. Buzzards, for example, initiated turns with subtle changes in the feathers on the edge of their wings, and turned by rolling their bodies left or right, the same way bicyclists lean into turns.

They two debated navigation and control systems for a glider, rejecting each idea as too heavy, cumbersome, unworkable, unreliable, or downright dangerous, until inspiration struck in the form of a cardboard box—a moment akin to Isaac Newton's apple.

A few weeks after Wilbur received a reply to his Smithsonian letter, he was working the counter of his bike store. After selling an inner tube, he played with the cardboard container while chatting with the customer. Suddenly he noticed if he squeezed the corners of the long, narrow box and twisted, the surfaces rotated in opposite directions. Immediately he envisioned a biplane. What if he could twist the wings as he did the box? By installing a cable that would pull the right wing up, the glider would experience more lift on that side while on the left it would decrease. It was the same principle that enabled buzzards to soar. The difference in lift would make the plane roll to the right or left. He christened the concept "wing warping."

Wilbur tested his theory on a biplane kite with a six-foot wingspan and a movable tail. He outfitted the kite with a system he could control from the ground with two sticks that allowed him to warp the wings. When he angled the sticks in opposite directions, the wings forced it to roll in the direction he thought it would. Watching were some boys from the neighborhood, who dove for cover whenever the kite swooped down on them.

Months later, in September 1900, the Wrights were in Kitty Hawk, North Carolina, on a quiet beach, a testing ground they chose for the frequent 15-mile-an-hour winds that swept the shore; the lack of trees, shrubs, and other hindrances; and its relative privacy. They spent the summer designing a glider with a ten-foot wingspan, melded out of a hodgepodge of parts, some of which they made and others they outsourced to Dayton craftsmen or customized from off-the-shelf merchandise. The frame was comprised of ash and spruce, with low-grade steel for the fittings, and braced with thick-gauge bicycle spoke wire. Wilbur had picked up the spruce for the wings from a lumberyard in Norfolk and sewn the wing tip covers from French satin, while the jumble of parts that formed the wing tips were scavenged from a small carriage.

In six weeks at Kitty Hawk and the nearby Kill Devil Hills, the Wrights measured the lift and drag generated by the glider while in flight, the first time this had ever been done, using sand bags, chains, and even a local boy as ballast. But they were discouraged with Wilbur's flights. In fact, his inaugural glide was almost his last. As his brother and a friend let out tension in the ropes, the glider rose into a stiff wind and then careened out of control. Wilbur screamed, "Let me down!" but they couldn't hear him. They assumed his aerial gymnastics were the product of his newfound piloting skill, and continued to let out more slack, which pushed the glider ever higher—until his hand motions became so frantic they realized he was in trouble and pulled him down.

The dozen other glides he took were barely better. Meanwhile, the craft took a beating. Like Lilienthal, who in his 2000 glides had been in the air for a little more than five hours total, Wilbur and Orville spent most of their time fixing the glider to get it air-worthy again after a crash.

The following summer they returned to North Carolina toting the parts for a new craft with double the wingspan— at the time, the largest glider ever made. It lacked lift and was prone to stalling, however, and when Wilbur—who at this point still did all the flying—attempted to warp the wings, he drifted sideways and fell into a nosedive, leaving him with more than his fair share of bruises and cuts and a deep gash in his forehead. By the time the brothers departed for home six weeks later, Wilbur was convinced that "not within a thousand years would man ever fly."

Nevertheless, they persisted. In Dayton, manifesting the old saying that an ounce of fact outweighs a pound of theory, they constructed their own wind tunnel from an old grinder and wood scraps and laboriously tested miniature models of wings at 45 different angles. Through this process, the first foray into aeronautical science, they learned that a wing produced far greater lift if its curve followed the shape of a parabola—that is, a v-shape with a softer edge.

In Kitty Hawk for their annual visit they found the new design vastly superior, achieving far greater lift, and traveling far greater distances—up to 500 feet on a glide. Orville also began to train as a pilot, and emulating his brother, wrecked the biplane, remarkably avoiding serious injury. The problem was the tail, which in turns didn't rotate fast enough. This time Orville came up with a solution: a moveable rudder that could be adjusted in flight. The new improvements made the glider much more stable, and the Wright brothers practiced their piloting skills by taking a hundred glides on some days and traveling 600 feet or more on occasion.

Satisfied that their flight and control problems were behind them, the Wrights turned their attention to the propulsion system, an eight-horsepower motor they calculated could not weigh more than 108 pounds. When no engine manufacturer was willing to make one based on these specifications, the brothers enlisted the aid of their bike store mechanic, Charlie Taylor. They didn't create detailed schematics. Instead, they would discuss it as a team and one of them would sketch out the part they wanted on scratch paper, and then Taylor would tack it over his bench and recreate it.

While Taylor busied himself with one end of the propulsion system, the brothers worked on the other. At first they assumed their propellers would be similar to a ship's, but soon realized they should be more akin to an airplane wing that spiraled. After much trial and error (and heated bickering, according to Taylor), Wilbur and Orville carved two eight-and-a-half-foot-long propellers from laminated spruce, wrapping the tips in canvas to prevent the wood from splitting. Through their wind tunnel tests, they estimated the propellers were 66 percent efficient in energy to thrust.

Some weeks later, Taylor cranked up the motor, which made such a racket neighbors raced in just in time to see gas fumes choking the mechanic. The next day its bearings iced over, and Taylor had to rebuild it. But he got it done. It wasn't pretty. In fact, it barely qualified as crude. The four-cylinder engine was set in a lightweight aluminum crankcase, cooled by water from a reservoir tank. Gasoline flowed from a small tank affixed to the wing. Perhaps the motor was more notable for what it lacked: no carburetor, fuel pump, spark plugs, or throttle, the initial spark being generated by four batteries stationed on the ground.

The Wright brothers traveled to Kitty Hawk in late September 1903 to construct their motorized biplane. Not far away, on the Potomac River near Quantico, Virginia, a competitor, Samuel Pierpont Langley, Secretary of the Smithsonian Institution, prepared to catapult a manned heavier-than-air machine equipped with an engine four times as powerful as the Wrights'. He christened it the *Great Aerodrome*, a 52-foot long, 48-foot wide ship forged from steel that sat atop a houseboat. For seven years, Langley, funded in part by the U.S. War Department, had been ex-perimenting with unmanned vessels equipped with en-gines—with mixed results. Some flopped, but two flew, his most successful "aerodrome" traversing more than 5000 feet. He believed that everything he had worked for was about to yield the glory he felt he deserved.

A little after noon on October 7, Charles Manley, Langley's co-designer who doubled as his mechanic, pulled himself on board the hulking vessel as reporters jostled for a clear view. Manley started the engine, and the *Aerodrome* skimmed across its 70-foot track until airborne, facing a gentle five-mile-an-hour breeze. It didn't get far before col-lapsing into a nosedive. Manley glanced down at the stop-watch strapped to his knee, noting he had been in the air barely two seconds before he shut down the engine and the ship flopped into the river. The *Great Aerodrome* disappeared under the waves until buoys urged it back to the surface. It had entered the water whole and re-emerged a sodden, mis-erable wreck. The wings hung like spaghetti, the propellers smashed to smithereens, the ship's frame a tangle of wiry carnage.

Manley, who had prudently clothed himself in a cork jacket, was fished from the river and rowed to shore in a small boat. While tugboats carted away the detritus, he changed out of his dripping wet clothes and offered a statement. Admitting that "the experiment was unsuccessful," Manley put on a brave face, claiming his "confidence in future success" was unhampered. Langley, who had visited the test site infrequently, wasn't even there. He heard the news in Washington.

The press was savage, bordering on cruel. Reporters nicknamed the once-majestic ship *The Buzzard*. One scribe remarked that the *Aerodrome* flew "like a handful of mortar." The *Chicago Daily Tribune* headline read: "Langley Airship a Total Failure. No Semblance of Flight in its Movement. Navigator Gets a Ducking." The *Los Angeles Times* said "Langley's Machine Flies to Smash." The *Washington Post* described it as a "costly contrivance utterly unable to take wing," while *The New York Times* called it "a ridiculous fiasco." Langley, for his part, refused interviews. He and Manley tried again on December 3rd, with even worse results. The *Aerodrome* split in two before hitting the water, and Manley, trapped in the skein of wires and steel, almost drowned. Five years later, after Langley passed on, some obituaries claimed he died of a broken heart.

Occupied with problems of their own, the Wrights didn't pay much attention to Langley's misadventures. By early November they had cobbled together the *Wright Flyer,* but the propeller shafts cracked the first time they juiced up the engine, and they sent the parts back to Dayton for

Charlie Taylor to fix. When they unwrapped the new propeller shafts a couple of weeks later, the sprockets wouldn't remain clamped to the shafts. A little hard cement fixed that. Then one of the renovated propeller shafts cracked. Orville carried it back to Dayton, where he constructed new ones from steel and then returned back to Kitty Hawk.

The brothers planned to test the *Flyer* on December 12, but there wasn't enough wind. The next day broke with ideal flying conditions, but it was Sunday, the Sabbath, a day of rest. On Monday, despite gentle skies and a soft, underwhelming breeze, they decided to risk it. After positioning the biplane on the edge of a 60-foot wooden rail and pointing it into the wind, Wilbur and Orville Wright flipped a coin to see who would go first.

Wilbur won. He assumed his position on the Flyer, and Orville and a small crew grabbed the wires leading to a battery and jolted the engine to life. Wilbur reached down to undo a wire holding the ship in place, but it was too tight, and the *Flyer* strained hard to move forward. To add slack, Orville and the crew pulled the plane back, and Wilbur unhooked it.

The ship shot up the ramp so fast that Orville couldn't keep up. About 45 feet after ignition the *Flyer*, living up to its name, rose eight feet above the track. Wilbur, not yet well versed with the controls, had begun his ascent too soon. By the end of the 60-foot ramp, he was 15 feet up. With the engine pounding, the plane stalled in mid air; the left wing swung down and gouged a hole into the sand. The *Flyer* pirouetted and crashed, the engine still running until Wilbur finally switched it off. Bitter failure was leavened by the realization that the *Flyer* had gotten off the track under its own steam. While they hadn't flown, they were confident they *could* fly. They telegrammed their father: "Misjudgment at start reduced flight... success assured keep quiet."

The plane was fixed in a few days, and then a nor'easter blew through and showered their camp with icy rain. Christmas was coming, and the brothers were growing impatient. Time was running out. Soon they would have to disband and return home.

On December 17, 1903, despite 30-mile-an-hour winds howling from the ocean and a wind chill factor of minus four, they decided to chance another test, even though they had never flown in such harsh conditions. After breakfast they hung a red banner on the side of the hangar—a signal to their support crew to help them prepare the plane for flight—and began laying the wooden track runway 200 yards from the cabin. Their crew materialized, helping them wrestle the quarter-ton flying machine across the frozen sand. By mid-morning the *Flyer* sat on the ramp.

Orville set up a tripod and camera and instructed 28-year-old John Daniels, *one* of the crew, to duck his head under the black cloth and squeeze the shutter just as the Flyer ran out of track. Then Wilbur and Orville each spun a propeller. The motor hacked and sputtered until it caught. Leaving the engine to warm, the brothers stepped aside for a moment of privacy. "After a while," Daniels later recalled, "they shook hands, and we couldn't help notice how they held on to each other's hand, sort o'like they hated to let go; like two folks parting who weren't sure they'd ever see each other again."

After shimmying his hips into the pilot's cradle and hooking the toes of his shoes on a supporting rack, Orville checked the controls—the wing warping mechanism, rudder, and "elevator," designed to urge the nose of the plane upward. Like his brother, he was dressed formally in a dark suit with a stiff collar, necktie, and a cap. While his brother fiddled with the controls, Wilbur addressed the crew gathered around the ramp. Their faces were grim, the air heavy with expectation; awed, they were, by the fact that they were about to witness history. To lighten the mood, Wilbur asked them to "laugh and holler and clap... to try to cheer Orville up."

A 27-mile-an-hour wind assailed Orville as he unlatched the restraining wire. Wilbur had kicked out the stool supporting the right wing, holding it in his hands. As the *Flyer* rumbled down the track, Wilbur ran alongside until the plane was moving too fast for him to keep up. Forty-five feet from the start, the plane lifted off to the cheers of the crew. Daniels squeezed the bulb and the flash went off, catching Orville and the contraption two feet above the ground.

The *Flyer's* nose pointed up too quickly, and Orville overcompensated by drawing the switch down, which caused the plane to pitch downward. Like Wilbur, he found the controls too sensitive; he needed the touch of a safecracker. Decades later, a computer simulation would show that a person needed a professional athlete's reflexes to keep the Wright Brothers' flying machine aloft. Yet that's precisely what Orville did. The *Flyer* fluttered up, down, up, down, Orville barely able to maintain control, until it came down 12 seconds and 120 feet later, the only damage a cracked skid.

After affecting repairs, the brothers took turns, each progressive flight covering greater distances, until Wilbur mounted the *Flyer* for the day's fourth trip. It started as haphazardly as the previous three, the plane undulating wildly soon after leaving the ramp. When it surpassed 300 feet, and with it Orville's best distance, Wilbur got the hang of it, and his flight path evened out 12 feet above the ground.

Knowing what he did about his chances of crashing, which were made even higher by the blustery wind, Wilbur capped his altitude to equal the height of two tall men. 400 feet, 500 feet, 600 feet... the *Flyer* continued on. Suddenly a sharp gust caught the plane, and it began its wild dance again. Wilbur tried to fight it, but the plane had other thoughts and came down 853 feet away, busting the elevator. When Orville, about a fifth of a mile away, checked the stopwatch, he found that Wilbur had been airborne for 59 seconds, averaging 31 miles per hour. Twelve seconds in the air might be considered a fluke, but not one minute minus one second.

Orville and the crew rushed to greet Wilbur, who waited alone in the cold, stunned by what he had accomplished. Meanwhile, Johnny Moore, a local boy, ran down the beach, kicking sand in his wake and yelling "They done it! They done it! Damned if they ain't flew," all the way to town.

Many had thought human flight impossible. Just eight weeks before, a *New York Times* editorial confidently asserted that a heavier-than-air machine with a human onboard was impossible. If it took a bird with rudimentary wings 1000 years to evolve to the point it could fly, or 10,000 years for a species with no wings that had to sprout them, to build a flying machine would require "the combined and continuous efforts of mathematicians and mechanicians" from "one million to ten million years." Langley's *Aerodrome* had, when all the bills were tallied, run almost $70,000. The Wrights, the ultimate do-it-yourselfers, did it for under $1,000, and that included all their travel, living expenses, and materials.

Returning the *Flyer* to the launch ramp with their crew, the Wrights mulled a four-mile flight to Kitty Hawk. When they put the plane down to rest, however, a giant gust scooped up one of the wings. With the *Flyer* about to capsize, Daniels grabbed a strut to pull it down, but the machine rolled over, taking him with it. Wood splintered, cloth ripped. Daniels, trapped in a web of sharp cables, was lucky he wasn't hurt. Now just scraps, this first *Flyer* would never fly again. But the Wrights would, and straight to immortality.

Initially, only four newspapers published articles about that day. The truth was that many journalists were skeptical. One perhaps apocryphal story has a newspaper editor, hearing of the Wright Brothers for the first time, saying, "Man will never fly, and if he does, he won't be from Dayton." In their hometown, their flights were greeted with equal skepticism. The city editor of the *Dayton Journal*, scoffed, "Fifty-seven seconds? If it were fifty-seven minutes it might be worth mentioning." When they applied for a patent, they faced more incredulity. So many had submitted plans and models for flying machines that the Patent Office had a stock answer: The plans were inadequate and the machine would never get off the ground.

The idea that Orville and Wilbur's flights were hoaxes took root, fueled in part by the brothers' stubborn obsession with secrecy, which was largely driven by their fear that their ideas would be stolen. The *Times of London* opined that all attempts at aviation "are not only dangerous to life, but foredoomed to failure from an engineering standpoint." *Scientific American* published "The Wright Aeroplane and its Fabled

Performances," in which editors laid out a case for why it would be impossible for the inventors to duck the press: "Is it possible to believe that the enterprising American reporter, who, it is well known, comes down the chimney when the door is locked in his face—even if he has to scale a fifteen-foot skyscraper to do so—would not have ascertained all about them and published... long ago?"

Skepticism spread far beyond America's borders. European newspapers were dismissive, with the French calling the Wright brothers *bluffeurs* (bluffers). "The Wrights have flown or they have not flown," read an editorial in the Paris edition of the *New York Herald*. "They possess a machine or they do not possess one. They are in fact either fliers or liars. It is difficult to fly. It's easy to say, 'We have flown.'" Another French paper derided "The Bluff Wright Brothers" that everybody has been talking about, but who as yet "have not made good."

This went on for five years, until 1908, when Wilbur offered a dazzling demonstration of his piloting skills in Paris that put the naysayers in their place. Afterwards the French press tripped over itself offering apologies. "The Wright brothers now should be as felicitated as they have been scoffed at," wrote one reporter. *Figaro* declared that Wilbur Wright's demonstration was a "triumph" that "creates revolution in the scientific world." The following year Wilbur took his final public flight around New York's Statue of Liberty, dazzling the throngs of people who caught sight of the famous flier and further cementing his place in history.

While the Wrights had become international heroes, their great engineering acumen did not extend to business.

They spent the next several years protecting their intellectual property, suing anyone who tried to follow in their footsteps for patent infringement. Their insistence that anyone manufacturing an airplane pay them a 20-percent royalty slowed down the pace of technological innovation in the United States. Until his death in 1912 from typhoid, Wilbur had been spending most of his time huddling with lawyers, and Orville blamed their patent struggles for his brother's early demise.

Sadly, the Wrights had long ceased to innovate and improve their aerial designs, and Orville sold the company he and his brother created for $250,000—enough money for him to never have to work ever again. When the United States entered the Great War in 1914, it was forced to purchase planes from foreign entities—namely Glen Curtiss, a Canadian-born entrepreneur who manufactured the JN-4 Jenny, the first mass-produced plane. It took the expiration of the Wright's patent in 1917 before American inventors jumped back into the fray.

By the early 1920's there were hundreds of companies building airplanes, many of them run by hobbyists out of woodsheds and spare rooms. It was during this mini-boom in aviation that Jack Northrop, a young, gruff mechanical engineering student, walked in on two brothers building a seaplane. They had no idea how to design a plane, so Northrop showed them some mathematics he'd picked up in engineering school, which helped them get their plane off the ground. They hired him and he worked on a number of early airplanes. When the company went bankrupt, he went to work at a small new airplane manufacturer called Lockheed, where he was instrumental in creating the Vega, the greatest plane of its era.

Named for the fifth brightest star visible from Earth, the Vega was faster than any other plane on the market, and could go 1000 miles before refueling—or 2500 miles if the cabin was modified to hold additional fuel tanks. Instead of the typical externally braced wing and fuselage designs of the late 1920s, the Vega was made out of a fabric-covered, molded plywood shell and internally braced cantilevered wings. This was a contentious design choice, since others believed the lack of external braces would drive off buyers afraid the plane wouldn't be sturdy enough. By putting the braces on the inside, however, the plane looked sleeker and cut wind drag, which meant it could go further without refueling. On the inside, the Vega's control panel was rudimentary: a fuel gauge, a turn-and-bank instrument, a vertical speed indicator, which would say if the plane were climbing or descending, a directional gyro, and windshield wiper controls pilots had to turn by hand. There was but a single engine and no brakes.

The first Lockheed Vega was christened the *Golden Eagle* and took its inaugural flight on July 4, 1927, a month and a half after Lindbergh crossed the Atlantic. Purchased by newspaper magnate George Hearst, it was entered into the Dole Air Derby only to disappear without a trace. Still, Lockheed Vegas quickly became the plane of choice for a generation of fliers: Amelia Earhart, Charles Lindbergh, Roscoe Turner, movie stuntmen Frank Tallman and Paul Manz, and, of course, Wiley Post and Jimmie Mattern, who left indelible marks on aviation history.

CHAPTER 6

Ticket to Siberia

June 3, 1933

JIMMIE MATTERN FELT AS IF HE HAD BEEN ASLEEP ABOUT
five minutes when a knock kick-started him awake, followed by a muffled voice from behind the door. "C'mon,
Jimmie. This is your big day."

The 28-year-old pilot bolted out of bed; he hadn't even
undressed from the night before. Planning to get to sleep
early, he had returned to Coney Island's Halfmoon Hotel
at seven p.m., but a pack of reporters trailed him through
the lobby and all the way to his room. He ordered a room
service dinner, which the newshounds treated as a solemn
occasion, although a few cracked "last supper" jokes under
their breaths. This wore on Mattern. He tried to clear the

room, but the reporters kept pushing for "just one more" question, while photographers' flashbulbs popped, etching electric blue tracers on the backs of his eyelids every time he blinked. Even with the window open, their cigarettes left a haze of smoke.

When he finally switched off the lights he was too jittery to sleep, tossing and turning until his sheets twirled in knots around his ankles. He filled time by running through a mental checklist. To neglect even the slightest detail, he knew, could be fatal. Finally, just as he was dozing off, the phone rang. It was his meteorologist, Dr. James H. Kimball, who informed him he would have clear skies and helping winds for the first 1200 miles, cold weather with perhaps some clouds to mid-ocean, and then storms the rest of the way to Ireland. He seemed to think there was a good chance Mattern would have westerly winds all the way across the Atlantic.

"That's good enough for me," said Mattern, who would fly blind and brave snow and rain if it meant a steady tailwind. He telephoned the field to order his plane made ready and then went back to bed while mechanics began fueling.

Mattern reasoned that three and a half hours of sleep was better than nothing. He slipped his flight suit over the same leather windbreaker and knickerbockers he wore on his flight with Griffin the year before. An hour later he was at Brooklyn's Floyd Bennett Field, a few steps from a completely refurbished *Century of Progress* painted red, white, and blue and festooned with a giant, menacing eagle. Well aware of Wiley Post's plans to girdle the earth alone—it had been in all the newspapers—he chose to lay low in hopes he could beat his wily rival to take off.

After the KGB had released Mattern and his friend following their last crash, they took their time traveling through Europe, figuring they ought to make the best of things. Mattern wasn't home more than a few days before his marriage began to unravel. Delia was tired of being married to an absentee husband, especially one already talking about another global expedition. Dangerous, record-setting attempts were hard on relationships. Harold Gatty's marriage disintegrated shortly after he got back from circling the world. The way Mattern saw it, it was either his wife or his airplane; and Mattern chose the plane. Delia moved back to Walla Walla to live with her sister, but she would play the dutiful wife whenever reporters came knocking. Neither wanted their troubles to make the newspapers.

Mattern's first step was to tap into Chicago's business community for backers. Because of the hundreds of newspaper column inches spilt on his ill-fated flight with Griffin, Mattern could leverage his minor celebrity status into access. Once face-to-face with a man, his natural charm and gift of gab took over. Even though the economy was even worse than the previous year, it didn't take long to sell the idea to Hayden R. Mills, secretary for the Mills Novelty Company, a manufacturer of slot machines, jukeboxes, and player pianos, and Harry B. Jameson, a partner in the Arrow Mill Co., a maker of wooden plates for storage batteries. Together they put in the lion's share of the $50,000 he needed. Then Mattern relocated to Brooklyn to take over a hangar at Floyd Bennett Field.

The *Century of Progress* arrived from Russia in two mammoth crates, and Mattern set out to rebuild it. An engineer at Standard Oil, Ed Aldrin, offered three spare Vegas sitting in a hangar from which Mattern could salvage parts. (Aldrin had a son named Buzz, who would grow up to be an astronaut and be the second man to step on the moon. When Buzz was a baby, Mattern would bounce him on his knee.) Mattern refurbished the engine and took tanks from his ship while grabbing a fuselage, wings, and tail from another plane that had once made a record flight to Buenos Aires. He visited Vincent Bendix of the Bendix Instrument Company and arranged to have everything on his console overhauled. Mattern lowered his landing gear and added shock cords to aid in rough landings and handle the weight of 702 gallons of fuel—enough to stay aloft for 28 hours. He installed a Hamilton convertible pitch propeller, which not only enabled him to start his own propeller without help from inside the cockpit but also improved fuel efficiency and increased speed. The final touches on the new *Century of Progress* included the patriotic paint job.

What he didn't have was a radio, deicers, or an automatic pilot, and since his Vega was a single engine monoplane, if the motor quit... he didn't want to think about it. Although Mattern was proud of the improvements, he believed technology paled to the man and that sheer force of will usually made all the difference.

The way Mattern saw it, he would fly across the Atlantic and beat Lindbergh's solo record to Paris—the technology had improved dramatically in six years—and then continue around the world. Even if he didn't break Lindbergh's or Post and Gatty's mark, he would still be the first solo pilot to circumnavigate the world. Since Post had pegged July 1 as his departure date, Mattern hoped to beat him to the air by a full month. That is, if the weather over the Atlantic would ever clear up. He had visited Dr. Kimball every single day for 30 straight days until the meteorologist finally gave the all clear. Thrill, fear, and apprehension flowed through him. While Mattern believed in himself and his abilities—and had suffered more than his fair share of close calls and scrapes with the angels—he also knew he might not make it back alive.

At Brooklyn's Floyd Bennett Field, Mattern slipped on his leather flight suit over the same leather windbreaker and knickerbockers he had worn on his flight with Griffin the year before. After driving to the runway, he jumped out of the car and ran the gauntlet of reporters, telling them, "I'll see you in about a week, I hope." Waving, he climbed into the cockpit and shouted, "So long, fellas!"

A representative from Pathé News, which was paying him to shoot photos to distribute exclusively over the wire, leaned in to hand him a 35-millimeter box camera, which Mattern stashed in a small storage bin built into his cramped cabin, joining six oranges, some Japanese green tea, and two gaily painted thermoses holding hot and cold water, one labeled "Happy" the other "Landings"—gifts from artist George Luks.

Mattern's mechanic had warmed the engine and parked the Vega, license number NR869E, at the extreme edge of the runway, its tail resting on the grass so that every available inch would be available for takeoff. The plane held almost double its weight in fuel, and Mattern wanted to be sure he could with all that extra weight still clear the expressway. If he couldn't, he would set the record for the shortest round-the-world attempt in history. Glancing around the airfield, he half expected his one-eyed friend and nemesis to sidle up next to him on the runway, but last he heard Post was still in Oklahoma City, struggling to retrofit his plane with finicky new technology. Mattern had won this stage of the race but knew his relief would be short-lived.

He revved the engine and nodded to the mechanics, who pulled away the wheel chocks. At precisely 4:40 a.m. the *Century of Progress*, gorged on gas, oil, and extra heavy expectations, started down the runway, gradually gaining speed. At 60 mph the wings bit into the westerly headwind and the tail came up. Mattern yanked the stick and the plane lifted clear, needing a little more than half of the 4000-foot runway. The fuel-laden ship rose 15 feet as it crossed a parking lot. Mattern pulled back on the stick as hard as he could and the plane struggled to clear Flatbush Avenue by 30 feet. Finally he coaxed it higher, and by the time he was over Jamaica Bay he was 1000 feet up, traveling at three miles a minute. He took a wide left bank turn and flew back over the airport and into the dawn sky. The cheering spectators below watched the *Century of Progress* fade into the Long Island haze as the red rim of the sun bled into the horizon.

On his way north, Mattern hugged the Eastern Seaboard, the weather joyously clear and a 15 mph tailwind urging him along. By the time he hit Harbor Grace, Newfoundland, he was ten minutes off Post and Gatty's pace, but since he didn't need to refuel he actually picked up a couple of hours. 100 miles northwest of the Great Circle course Lindbergh had followed, Mattern's plane was spotted near Lewisporte. Next he was heard over Fogo Island, in Notre Dame Bay, where his engine's roar startled several fishermen. By late afternoon he was sighted over the tiny Wadham Islands, off the extreme northeastern coast of Newfoundland, the last evidence of land Mattern would see before Europe.

But something wasn't right. While land was in sight, he hadn't bothered to mark his position on the map and check his route because he had flown the same route less than a year earlier. Now that he was over open sea, his compass was telling him he was several degrees off course. Sipping hot tea, it occurred to him the vacuum-packed thermoses might be magnetized. Scowling, he smashed the one labeled "Happy" and then the other—"Landings"—and stuffed their shards through the tiny window. The compass remained off kilter. He couldn't figure out what could be causing it until his eye settled on the boxy 35mm camera Pathé News had given him. Mattern snatched it off the shelf and passed it from his left hand to his right, watching the compass needle follow the camera's path. The needle tracked it when he passed it the other way, too. Mattern rapped the camera body with his knuckles. *Metal!* He had run through what he thought was every possible detail and now this? The windows were too small to ditch the camera. He was trapped with it. All he could do was move it from one side of the cockpit to the other every 15 minutes and hope he didn't veer too far off course, run out of fuel, and vanish without a trace.

He might as well forget Paris. Hell, he would be lucky to locate the European continent. Less than a third of the way across the ocean, he smacked into whiplash turbulence, gale force winds, and pelting rain. He climbed to 6000 feet to rise above it. Inside the cockpit Mattern was shivering; if he spit the gob would freeze before it hit his shoes. With ice forming on his wings, he pushed his plane's nose down. Seeking warmer air, he tried different altitudes and directions, veering south, and when that didn't work, turning north. He dove deeper into the storm's heart to within 100 feet of the water, afraid he might plow the surf at any moment.

Suddenly there was a sickening sound from outside. He realized one of his wings had cracked. Heart racing, his face went white. *I guess I'm going to join all of the others that tried and didn't make it.* He thought of his mother, sitting by the radio in Dallas, waiting for word of her son, and his father, long gone from this earth. Miraculously the wing held. The wooden frame complained but didn't break, and Mattern's plane droned on.

For ten hours he battled the swirling North Atlantic storm, struggling to keep the ship on the straight and narrow as he hurtled through rain, snow, sleet, and turbulent skies as darkness enveloped him. He was flying blind, relying strictly on his instruments, and chastising himself every time he was a minute or two late repositioning the metal camera, which he continued to do every quarter hour. One night felt like a year. The strain was enormous, and it added to his fatigue.

Along this same route, lack of sleep had almost been Charles Lindbergh's undoing. Seventeen hours after leaving New York, he'd lost control of his eyelids. "My back is stiff; my shoulders ache; my face burns; my eyes smart," Lindbergh wrote in *The Spirit of St. Louis*, his recounting of his journey. "It seems impossible to go on longer. All I want in life is to throw myself down flat, stretch out—and sleep." Twenty-four hours into his aerial trek, Lindbergh began to hallucinate.

The last time Mattern had flown the Atlantic, Bennett Griffin had shared piloting duties. This time he was on his own. Sleep deprivation could be as dangerous as any lightning storm. It could lead a good pilot to make bad decisions or black out at inopportune times. The *Washington Post*, in its coverage leading up to Mattern's global trek, reported that the Texas birdman had no fear of falling asleep because "if he dozes off, and the plane falls, a gadget fastened on to an altimeter squirts water when the plane tumbles down to a minimum altitude of safety." Perhaps this was Mattern or Griffin having fun at the expense of a gullible reporter. In reality, Mattern's system was much more prosaic. He attached rubbed bands to the stick from his console so the ship would list slightly to the right, and then he crossed his legs and pushed down on the left rudder with his right foot to equalize the drift. This kept the *Century of Progress* on an even course while Mattern took quick catnaps—not that he could take one in the eye of a storm. During severe weather like this, fear alone was enough to keep him wide-eyed and on edge.

Twenty hours into his flight he finally made it to the other side of the storm. Calculating the amount of fuel he had left, he knew he would be cutting it close. He checked the emergency reserve 70-gallon tank Amelia Earhart had given him as a going-away gift. As soon as one of his five main tanks went dry he planned to switch to the reserve tank, but when he tested it the engine quit. Something was blocking the fuel from injecting into the motor. He made the switch back to one of the big tanks until it ran dry and tried again. Still the engine couldn't draw the fuel from the reserve. Mattern was going to need that tank. It wasn't like he could pull off to the side of the road to repair it.

Leaning into the rising sun, Mattern finally spotted land on the horizon. His last large fuel tank was almost dry, and in desperation he flipped the switch to the reserve tank. The engine coughed, stopped, and then kicked on again. Later he would learn a small piece of felt had lodged in the line. It was pushed farther down and toward the engine each time he turned on the gas until it was finally forced through.

As sea gave way to land, Mattern realized he hadn't seen a ship since leaving Jamaica Bay. Flying over mountains and glaciers, he wondered how far north he had ventured. With no airfields and only a few minutes left of fuel, he searched for a place to land. He circled a small island with a sandy beach and sunbathers frolicking in the surf and then cut the engine to bring the *Century of Progress* down in a glide. When he got closer, he realized too late that he was coming down on loose stones, some of them as big as boulders. He prepared for the worst, not sure if he would be able to keep the plane from flipping over or barreling into the sea. Even if he'd had brakes, he wasn't sure it would have been wise to deploy them. It was a bumpy, teeth-chattering ride as his wheels struck rocks, gravel, and sand. Mattern thanked his foresight in installing shock chords on the landing gear. Even so the rough landing knocked the tail out of alignment, and he blew a tire when it rammed into a boulder.

Mattern checked his watch. He had shaved ten hours off the 33 hours Lindbergh took to cross the Atlantic. Elated, he squirreled through the hatch and sank to his knees on the beach as a score of sunbathers greeted him.

"I just flew nonstop from New York," Mattern told them. "I am trying to make the first solo flight around the world and break the existing speed record. I need your help."

No one spoke English. Exhausted, Mattern was practically carried to a nearby summer cottage where he met someone with whom he could communicate.

He learned he was in Jomfruland, Norway, 80 miles from Oslo and 1000 miles north of Paris, where he had intended to land. Mattern told the translator he wanted gas and oil so he could be on his way, but the man urged him to rest while he dispatched a message to Oslo. While Mattern napped, a seaplane arrived with Captain Hoever, chief of the Norwegian airport in nearby Horten. With him were a couple of his mechanics and supplies of gasoline and oil. Capt. Hoever was astonished that any airman could have landed on that beach without wrecking his craft. In addition to the misaligned landing gear and blown tire, flying stones had damaged one of the wingtips during the landing. There was also a more serious gash in one of the wings, which Mattern surmised had been struck by lightning.

It took Capt. Hoever and his mechanics four hours to mend the plane and pump it with enough fuel for Oslo, where Mattern could gorge his tanks for the long haul to Moscow. Mattern didn't want to seem ungrateful, but he was determined to return the sky. The captain, however, convinced him to grab a little more sleep and wait for dawn. It also afforded him the luxury of a bath and shave.

As the sun rose at 3 a.m., Mattern made his way to his plane. Horses had pulled it to a grassy knoll so that repairs could be affected. With no brakes, the Vega was tied to a couple of boulders that were pinned in front of the wheels. When Mattern revved the engine, Capt. Hoever and the mechanics pulled the rocks free and the *Century of Progress* started rolling. The beach was too rough to take off from, so Mattern taxied down the knoll.

He was alarmed to see his makeshift runway pockmarked

with sandpits, each large enough to swallow a wheel. One errant move and his trip would be over. Mattern sped on anyway and witnessed a remarkable sight: a Norwegian waist deep in each hole, waving his arms frantically and operating as human traffic cones. Mattern swerved around the first, then another, another, the men marking each wheel-swallowing obstacle with their bodies and flapping arms, the tips of his propeller coming dangerously close. *Brave people*, Mattern thought.

It was a short hop to Oslo, where Mattern handed the camera to the airport manager to ship to New York. Since standard capacity for a Vega was 100 gallons, Mattern had to show him the extra-large fuel tanks before he would allow him 400 gallons of fuel. At 6:40 a.m. Mattern started on his 1100-mile trek to Moscow, drawing a straight line across Sweden, the Baltic Sea, Estonia, and Latvia.

Airfields in Europe had been awaiting news of his whereabouts. Crowds maintained a ceaseless vigil at Le Bourget field in Paris. As the hours clicked away, fear turned to despair with the realization that Mattern must have run out of fuel. Reluctantly the Le Bourget dispatcher switched off the floodlights that had burned through the night. Weary newsmen at Berlin's Tempelhof airport dragged themselves off to bed. In England telephone operators made last efforts to raise remote stations. Wireless stations as far away as Spain were on the alert. Several coastal towns in Ireland claimed to have spotted the wayward flier. Western Union operators at Valentia, Ireland, identified his plane over their heads at 8:15 a.m., while other witnesses said it was flying too high to be identifiable. At 9:30 a.m., the steamer *Hastings* in the English Channel reported an eastbound plane overhead.

Later another message—this time from Kilgarvan in County Kerry—indicated that Mattern had been flying in a south-westerly direction, which would have led him to open sea.

"MATTERN MISSING ON WORLD FLIGHT," cried a *New York Times* headline. "Eighteen hours overdue on the first stage of his world flight, James Mattern is feared to have been lost somewhere in the Atlantic." Another *Times* headline added, "LONDON FEARS ACCIDENT." The article noted that Mattern's "fuel should have been exhausted at noon yesterday." The *Boston Globe* reported that "MOSCOW HAS NO WORD FROM AMERICAN FLIER," while the Spartanburg *Herald Journal* said that "SILENCE SWALLOWS AMERICAN AVIATOR HEADED FOR PARIS." The *L.A. Times* speculated that "Mattern either went to the graveyard of trans-Atlantic flyers on the first lap of his attempt to fly around the world alone, or was fished from the sea by a steamer without wireless, or landed today in some wilderness far from communication with the outside world." His manager, Jack Clark, ventured that his exhausted client might have landed in a remote corner of Ireland or France and fallen asleep in his plane, but when almost 48 hours had passed, he allowed that he might have met with trouble.

Delia Mattern, "the young and attractive wife of Jimmie Mattern," with her "blonde hair in perfect order" and "light brown eyes showing just a hint of anxiety," told an obviously bewitched Associated Press reporter that her husband had landed in rough places before. "Anyway, I never give up hope and I won't," she said. She hadn't seen her husband since March in Chicago, and Mattern wasn't one to write letters. She had never understood his daring air escapades.

She would ask him if he was afraid and Mattern would re-
tort, "Of course I'm not afraid. If I were I wouldn't be going."
He didn't seek her counsel. He did things his own way. She
claimed the strain was worse on the wife who stays home
knitting than on the pilot.

It wasn't until Mattern swooped down from angry clouds
on to Moscow's muddy field that the world, save for a gaggle
of Norwegians sunbathers and a few airport personnel in
Oslo, learned of his whereabouts. After taxiing, he was gathered up by half a dozen Soviet aviators and tossed into the
air several times in celebration. Noting several familiar faces
among the correspondents covering his surprise arrival, he
said, "It seems almost like being back home again." He had
completed a third of his journey in 51 hours and 31 minutes,
three hours faster than Post-Gatty's record time.

When a reporter told him many feared he had been lost,
Mattern grinned. "Fooled 'em, didn't I?"

He was escorted to the airdrome reception room where
he requested gasoline and oil. Officials, in return, filled
him in on weather conditions and landing facilities east of
Moscow. An airport physician felt his pulse and remarked,
"He is very tired and needs rest." Mattern brushed off the
doctor's warning, promising to take a two-hour nap before
lifting off again. Regaling reporters with the story of his
mysterious disappearance, he ate sparingly of a sumptuous
spread laid out in his honor—caviar, cold cuts, omelet, sal-
ad, steak, and mineral water, and drank several glasses of
Russian tea. A shower, a shave, a nap; and then, with a crew
of Soviet mechanics, he worked on his plane under a bright
spotlight.

As they put the finishing touches on his cracked wing,

Mattern joined a group of Russian pilots inside to talk over his Siberian route, ate an orange, and sipped more tea. His maps were virtually useless—they showed only a few lakes, mountains, and settlements. A guard was supposed to be watching his ship, but when Mattern looked outside he saw people swarming all over it. They seemed particularly enamored with his metal propeller. Mattern was afraid someone was going to pull off a chunk as a souvenir. He ran out, gunned the engine, and took off into the eastern moonlight shortly after midnight of his third day. Destination: Omsk.

Looping over the Ural Mountains, he weathered a lightning storm that cracked electric whips, and then, following the tracks of the Trans-Siberian railway, he made a beeline across unending flatlands, battling vicious headwinds and temperatures that careened from zero to 100 degrees Fahrenheit. At full throttle he managed only 120 mph, and it took 12 hours and 21 minutes to cover 1400 miles of monotonous landscape. Dropping out of the sky in Omsk, he was so tired that he carelessly came down too hard and cracked his right landing strut. He took a sauna and then slept on the ground beside the ship for three hours while the strut was fixed and the plane refueled.

When he awoke he got on the phone with a *New York Times* reporter in Moscow, who informed him he was only a few hours behind Post and Gatty's time. "That's great!" Mattern shouted into the static, his voice hoarse. "I'll beat 'em yet."

Despite a brisk tailwind, the pace was beginning to wear on him and his plane. A third of the way to Irkutsk, Mattern's eyelids began to droop and he was having trouble breathing. His head was spinning, and the control panel got all zig-zaggy. He caught a whiff of gasoline and began to retch. His last conscious thought was that a fuel line had broken, but he couldn't let go of the controls. The *Century of Progress* plummeted to earth, its pilot oblivious.

Mattern regained consciousness to the groaning of his engine in free fall and the ground rushing at him. He pulled back on the stick as hard as he could and somehow lifted the craft's nose. There was nothing but miles of trees below. Mattern opened his window and then turned the bus on its side to maximize the amount of air coming in. He let the wind brush against his face and blow back his hair, trying to keep himself from vomiting all over the cockpit.

Finally he spotted a field that looked smooth enough, although landing there would still be tricky. To keep his saggy stabilizer steady, he had stashed an additional 300 pounds of fuel in the tail. One false move would mean a quick and fiery finish. Mattern coaxed the *Century of Progress* down until the wheels skimmed the dirt. By the time the ship rolled to stop, he was unconscious again. The next thing he knew, Russian peasants had climbed into the plane and were trying to yank him out of his safety harness. They were pure white from the eyebrows up, as though, Mattern thought, there was no circulation in the brain area. Apparently they hadn't seen too many planes before and gawked at the strange pilot in his leather flight suit.

Coughing from the fumes, Mattern shouted blood-curdling obscenities while unclasping himself and then chased them from the cockpit. He staggered from the ship under his own power, but once his feet touched earth his legs buckled. One of the peasants, about Mattern's height and twice as wide, caught him. Mattern locked eyes and told him, "You keep those boys from jumping all over that plane, see, and don't let them take any souvenirs." Miraculously, the man understood.

His new friend, whom Mattern took to calling "No. 1 Assistant," tapped another man to guard the ship and half-dragged the wobbly flier to a low wooden shack. Mattern thought at first it might be a barn but realized it was someone's home. Lying on a bunk he once again felt his world whirl out of control. Retching until there was nothing left in his stomach, he retched some more. Strange faces, all talking in a language he didn't comprehend, taunted him. Finally, toward evening, he felt well enough to stand, and No. 1 Assistant helped him to his plane parked in a cow pasture and surrounded by dozens of Siberians pop-eyed and waiting to help.

Waiting for him was a short, stocky man about 50 years old who spoke fluent English. He had a short gray beard and reminded Mattern of General Grant. Mattern learned he had been mixed up in a Montana labor fight before the Great War, and when he got out of prison he made his way to Belovo, Russia—where Mattern had landed—and was a foreman at a non-ferrous metal-refining plant. General Grant was an apt nickname, and when Mattern told him what he needed, the general ordered the crowd around, getting the airplane pulled out of the mud patch where it had pancaked and hoisting the tail up on a giant post driven into the ground. Mattern could see that it was in bad shape, in need of extensive repairs. With tools and material from the nearby factory, workers began tacking sheet metal to the tail until early the next morning, when a plane arrived with the chief engineer from Novosibirsk airport and his assistant.

They worked in pouring rain inside a roped-off square; like a prizefight, Mattern thought, with soldiers with fixed bayonets guarding the ship and about half of the local population watching with mouths open as if they were attending a circus. Towering over everyone was a hulking guard—Mattern guessed he might be from Mongolia—with a gargantuan fur hat like the kind worn at Buckingham Palace, only his was spicy mustard yellow. He stood for 12 hours, stiff and solemn as a statue. Toward dusk the rain stopped; they continued working with light cast by big flares of cotton waste soaked in oil. The crowd, instead of going home, just got bigger, as if this was their evening entertainment. Mattern tried to eat but nothing would stay down, although he could feel the gas fumes sweating out of his system.

With repairs complete, the *Century of Progress* looked two-thirds modern airship and one-third junkyard heap. Mattern figured it would fly lopsided but hold together long enough to reach Krasnoyarsk, which was several hundred miles away. Drenched by the rain, the field, however, was mush. Mattern traipsed out a couple of hundred yards with the general and the mechanics from Novosibirsk shaking their heads. "*Nyet, nyet,*" they said.

Determined to do whatever it took, Mattern lightened his gas load to a minimum and started the motor, but the wheels wouldn't bite. He just couldn't raise enough speed. His Russian helpers laid down ashes and sacking, mobilizing the entire crowd, who seemed pleased to do more than just watch. But he couldn't pull his ship out of the slop. They huddled together, with Mattern suggesting they move the plane to higher ground where it was drier. It would be a very short runway that ran into a wedge of tall trees.

The Russian pilot grunted "*nyet*"—not for a bus of this size—but Mattern swore he would fight it out if it took all summer. After they towed the craft to its new resting place, Mattern hopped in and started the motor. With no brakes, he would either make it or crash. The ship started rolling, Mattern's eyes glued to the bank of trees. As he picked up speed he felt enmeshed in a game of chicken with a stationary target. Heart pattering in his chest, he pulled back on the stick. The *Century of Progress* touched off the ground just in time, the landing gear brushing against the tops of the trees.

As he gained altitude his plane, its tail dipped in gobs of molten metal, flew steadier than Mattern felt. He had tried to eat breakfast before taking off but it wouldn't stay down, adding to the days he had gone without eating. More rain and fog cut visibility until four hours out of Belovo, when he saw sunshine for the first time in practically a week. Mattern slid open the window for fresh air and sighted a large sugar-loaf-shaped mountain, which he had been told was 50 miles beyond where he was headed. The mountains looked awfully good to Mattern after traveling over thousands of miles of flatland steppes. Flipping the ship around, he coasted along railway tracks until he could make a nice, easy landing at the airfield.

Mattern stayed just long enough to fuel up for the long haul to Irkutsk and then Khabarovsk, which was 2000 miles east and housed a major military installation. There he booked a hotel room and fell asleep almost immediately, as mechanics readied his battered ship for the haul across the Bering Sea to Nome, Alaska; then, he hoped, home.

When he awoke, Soviet military pilots advised him to fly

their regular air route, which would take him across lower Siberia, but Mattern insisted on taking a northerly route to shave time off his journey. When the pilots warned him that the Pacific hop was dangerous even in the best of conditions, Mattern replied, "The Atlantic wasn't so hot, and Siberia hasn't proved so lucky either." He hoped he would have better luck riding those Pacific waves.

He didn't. The first time he left Khabarovosk he struck headwinds, rainstorms, and dense clouds that made it hard to navigate. As night fell and the sky turned inky black, Mattern lost his way and realized he was running low on oil. The Russian oil was cruder and burned a lot faster. At this point he didn't even care what lay below. He stacked pillows around his head and brought the Vega down in a surprisingly smooth landing. After cutting the switch, he climbed out of the hatch and jumped eight feet down to mother earth, where he promptly fell asleep.

At dawn, Mattern was astonished to find his ship teetering on a sand bar overlooking the river, across from a small village. A boat of peasants was rowing toward him bringing eggs, fish, and black bread, which Mattern couldn't stomach. He pantomimed that his plane needed oil. Although no one spoke English, one of the peasants was a former pilot in the Soviet army, and dispatched a wagon the 13 miles to a farm cooperative, where they "borrowed" what Mattern needed. He started his abused Wasp engine, which smoked from the change in diet—the oil he secured was for tractors, not airplanes—and returned to Khabarovsk.

At 4 a.m. the next morning he tried again. This time heeding the Soviet pilots' advice, he followed a more southerly route over the Okhotsk Sea, but 500 miles over open water, ice clawed at his wings; it was even worse than it had been over the Atlantic. He couldn't shake it off even after practically skimming the water. Worse, there was thick fog. He decided to return to Khabarovsk again, dumping 450 gallons of fuel before landing. Mattern had flown 1400 miles yet hadn't gained an inch. Back with the Soviet pilots, he replenished himself with a couple of hearty meals and eight hours sleep. Although he was far behind Post and Gatty's time, he congratulated himself that he was still on track to be the first pilot to fly solo around the world. All he had to do was make it this last leg across Siberia and the 500 miles of choppy water known as the Bering Sea. Once he hit Alaska he would be home free.

Mattern waited through two more days of dirty weather before revving up his engine. This time he crossed the frozen Okhotsk Sea and came to the Kamchatka Peninsula at the edge of the Arctic Circle, where there were 8000-foot mountains. He couldn't fly over them because his wings would ice up. Instead he wove through the passes and over the lower ranges. It was stinging cold, but Mattern warmed himself with the knowledge that he had covered 1900 miles of the 2500-mile stretch of this leg. Nome, Alaska lay about four hours to the east over the Bering Sea.

Suddenly he noticed his oil gauge pointing to empty. The oil he had accepted from the Soviet collective was clogging his lines, giving his finely tuned Wasp engine heartburn. He had a reserve supply stashed in the back with a bicycle pump jerry rigged to push oil to the engine, except it had frozen.

He was losing engine power with hundreds of miles of open water ahead and knew he wasn't going to make it. His dream of being the first to fly solo around the world was about to come to a crashing halt. Below was almost endless wasteland, most likely uninhabited, certainly inhospitable and forbidding. Drawing on his bush pilot experience, Mattern followed the little streams because he knew they usually led to rivers, and rivers to settlements, and then hopefully to the Anadyr River. The crash from the year before near Minsk flashed through his mind. He would almost certainly tip over if he came down on such tough terrain, and this time there would be no one to dig him out.

There was only one thing he could do. It was going to be tricky because he had almost no margin for error.

Mattern opened the throttle all the way and accelerated to the Vega's top speed, 200 mph. Skimming over the frozen tundra, he sheered off his landing gear and then brought the ship to earth, belly-flopping like a giant sled on the snow. The plane bounced and shook. Mattern heard the wing crack from the stress and was afraid the entire undercarriage would tear apart. As the plane slowed, the searing hot engine was forced back almost into his lap and he felt a sharp pain in his ankle. It seemed an eternity but had only been a minute or so when he came to a complete stop. Somehow the *Century of Progress*—and Mattern—had held together.

His heart pounding, the marooned pilot leaned back in his seat and closed his eyes. After a few deep breaths, he said a quick prayer and freed his wounded ankle. Not a clean break—the bones didn't look like they had pulled apart—but he was sure it was fractured. After staggering out of the hatch he looked around.

He hadn't seen a soul in a thousand miles, and there was barren tundra as far as the eye could see. His plane was a wreck. Wind whistled by his ears and he shivered. Never had he felt so alone.

He was alive. For that he was grateful. But he knew he couldn't last long. Being summer and lit by the sun more than 20 hours a day, this was as warm as it got. In a few months, it would turn inhospitably cold. And unless he found food, he would, sooner than that, end up like so many other pilots who had tried and failed.

Only his death wouldn't be quick and glorious as in a fiery crash. It would be slow and agonizing.

CHAPTER 7

Malfunction Junction

July 15, 1933

BEFORE DAWN CREPT OVER JAMAICA BAY, WILEY POST ambled to the airport register that logged every outgoing flight and signed his name. In the next box he scribbled, "From Floyd Bennett Field. Destination same." On his way past throngs of well-wishers held back by police tape to the *Winnie Mae*, Post fingered an old red medal another pilot had given him that had once been owned by Count Felix von Luckner, a World War I German naval officer famous for never suffering casualties. As Post watched mechanics pour five gallons of heated oil into his plane's engine, Mae, his wife, slender and silent, stood nearby while a throng of people behind ropes cheered.

"Are you about gone?" she asked.

"Pretty soon," he said.

"Be careful."

"I will."

These few words and a kiss were all the parting. She tried not to let her fears get the best of her. Jimmie Mattern's disappearance had set her nerves on edge, but Wiley reassured her. His plane had every possible modern innovation. One reason it had taken so long to get off the ground was that he had been in Dayton, Ohio, where the Army Air Corps installed a radio transmitter. The technology was so new the Army insisted on providing armed guards to watch his ship. It would enable him to fix his position from broadcasts on ordinary wavelengths just by knowing the call letters of the radio station doing transmitting. He was also counting on his Sperry automatic pilot to do much of the flying for him—the first time a civilian aircraft had been outfitted with one—and his Smith controllable-pitch propeller to shorten take off runs and squeeze every last mile out of his fuel. By secreting additional tanks in the wings, he increased his range so that he could accomplish the journey in five stops, starting with a direct flight from New York to Berlin.

This, he believed, was what separated him from Mattern. Post courted new technology—which was odd when he thought about it, given his rural upbringing, Oklahoma drawl, and down-home ways. Mattern, on the other hand, flew by the seat of his pants, as loquacious in flight as he was in life. In his rush to take off first, he had not considered the effects that sleep deprivation could have on a man, nor had he properly outfitted his plane to address this. Post reckoned his friend's plane had likely come apart over the Bering

Straits, accelerated by the poor decision-making that was the inevitable byproduct of saturating fatigue.

To most people, Post knew he came across as an uneducated hick, but he was only one of two men in the world who knew what it took to circle the globe. He was leaving nothing to chance. Just in case, Post also incorporated decidedly less high-tech measures. He planned to tie a string around his finger and to the other end attach a wrench. If he fell asleep and his hand slipped off the stick, the wrench would clang to the floor and wake him.

In his natty new gray suit with blue shirt and tie, Post climbed into the cockpit. "I'll be back as quick as possible," he shouted. He gave the word and the motor buzzed to life, the propeller sending gravel flying. Onboard were 659 gallons of fuel, quart size thermos bottles of water and tomato juice, three packages of chewing gum, a package of zwieback (a crispy, sweet bread), a knife, a hatchet, a raincoat, a cigarette lighter, mosquito netting, a sleeping bag, and a pocket searchlight. He also brought fishing tackle. If he were marooned in Siberia, he could always fish for food. He had a few changes of clothes, including three fresh eye patches his wife had sewn and which he carried in a suitcase, and one other piece of equipment he hadn't bothered with last time: a parachute.

Mae Post hastened to another Lockheed Vega, which her brother owned. She was going to follow her husband for the first couple of miles. The plane quickly took off and circled the airfield, waiting for the *Winnie Mae* to lead the way. Post's WASP engine crescendoed, spewing exhaust. He signaled to pull the chocks from the wheels and the plane began to roll. In the distance, a crimson-streaked dawn unfolded with a glowing half moon overhead. The white and purple monoplane picked up speed over the concrete runway, and despite the heavy load, quickly climbed. Mayor J. Nelson Keely, manager of the port and official timer, announced the takeoff time as 5:10:10 a.m.

The *Winnie Mae* was 300 feet over Jamaica Bay as the ship carrying Post's wife tagged along. Soon both faded into the clouds hanging over the water. Half an hour later, Mrs. Post's plane touched down. She reported what her pilot had told her: The *Winnie Mae* was on her way, traveling 155 mph at an altitude of 1000 feet.

It didn't take Post long to catch up to a front of clouds and fog. He climbed to 1200 feet to wing over the top, where it was frigid in his unheated cockpit. After two hours he came down to a more manageable altitude, where he wouldn't have to worry about ice settling on his wings. He turned on the autopilot, which eased much of the strain of flying. When Post hit Newfoundland he picked up a radio station at St. John's to get a fix on his position. He learned the weather would be clear until halfway to England, which was what Dr. Kimball had forecast.

Like Mattern, about 12 hours into his transoceanic flight he encountered tempestuous weather, and again jumped to two miles above sea level. He kept his radio on until he heard "a special broadcast for Wiley Post" from station G2L0, Manchester, England, which cut through the static. Post adjusted his radio compass needle to get a fix on the station and then picked up additional stations as he flew over the Irish Sea to the British Isles and to the Continent. He was flying blind, yet had never been so secure in his location.

The weather gradually improved and Post sighted land

as he passed over the Elbe River. Ahead was Berlin's skyline. When he landed at Templehof airdrome, 25 hours and 40 minutes after he had left New York, he had not only broken Mattern and Bennett's time by almost four hours, he had accomplished the first non-stop flight from New York to Berlin, 3,942 miles—also a record. As Post taxied up the runway, the American flag and German national colors floated above the field. Steel-helmeted Nazi storm troopers with rifles kept 2000 cheering Germans at bay. One of those in attendance: Commander-in-Chief of the Luftwaffe, Hermann Goering. Unlike the last time Post touched down at Templehof, there was no mob scene.

Post, assisted by a policeman, climbed down while a band played "The Star Spangled Banner" and Nazi anthems. He was tired but managed a fake smile for the oncoming wave of photographers, newsmen, and airport officials. The first thing he said was, "I want to get this gassed up and get going as quick as possible." Greeters offered beer and food, but Post was all business. "I don't want to eat. I don't want to shave. I just want to clear out of here. I flew here on tomato juice and chewing gum, and that's enough for me." He was nettled because he'd thought he could make it across in 22 hours, but fog, snow, and ice had slowed him down. Post was whisked off to the same room where he had rested on his first flight, stood for nearly 20 minutes under a cold shower, and then stretched out on a bunk.

He tried to clear his mind, to shut down for a few minutes before tearing into the sky again, but he was restless. A lot of people were depending on him. In early 1933, Post had inked an agreement with a local Oklahoma City businessman to line up investors in exchange for a ten-percent cut of any and all fees he raised. Wary of reliving his troubled relationship with F.C. Hall, Post insisted on a pool of investors, avoiding any one person acquiring too much influence. The Oklahoma City Chamber of Commerce, mindful of Post's fame and local hero status, eagerly formed a committee.

Money trickled in slowly at first, until the managing editor of the *Oklahoma City Times* heartily endorsed the flight, appealing to Oklahomans' civic pride. Eventually, 41 businesses and individuals contributed. Post approached aeronautical companies for donations of equipment, support and supplies. Mobil gave him oil, gas, and grease, while the Sperry Gyroscopic company donated its new automatic pilot. Pratt & Whitney provided parts for the WASP engine, and the U.S. Military came through with a radio transmitter that could track his location. The Roosevelt Hotel in New York offered a suite and half-off on food for Post and his team before departure and after returning home.

In late March, Post flew from Oklahoma City to Mexico City and back to test the Sperry autopilot, which he nicknamed "Mechanical Mike." A few weeks later Post invited his friend Luther E. "Red" Gray, a pilot for Braniff Airways, to take the *Winnie Mae* for a quick spin to show him the latest features. Gray pointed out that the fuel gauge pointed to empty, but Post said it must be busted because he hadn't flown since partially filling the tank. There was, Post assured, plenty of gas for a short trip.

With two additional passengers on board, Gray raced down the runway at the airfield just south of Chickasha, Oklahoma, and gently pulled back on the stick. 50 feet in the air, the engines abruptly cut out and the plane dropped like an anvil out of the sky. An experienced flier, Gray pulled up the nose and guided the wounded ship back to earth, managing a miraculously solid landing. Having no brakes, the Vega quickly ran out of runway, plowing into a peach orchard and colliding with 20-foot trees. Those inside the plane were tossed about, with Post slicing open his finger, while another passenger cracked two ribs. The *Winnie Mae*, ravaged by the crash, was less fortunate. The six-ply plywood cabin was smashed and splintered in sections, a wing cracked, landing gear askew. At first Post suspected sabotage, but it turned out a couple of teenagers had, the night before, siphoned gas out of the tanks for their car.

The plane was transported to Oklahoma City, where Gray enlisted a crew of ace Braniff mechanics led by George Brauer, a master woodworker from Germany, who oversaw the bodywork. Meanwhile, a Pratt & Whitney technician arrived to oversee the overhaul of the engine. In addition to extensive repairs and refurbishments, Brauer's team installed larger fuel tanks, which raised the plane's carrying capacity to 654 gallons, and added a special pump designed to balance the liquid load. This prevented fuel from sloshing around during turbulence or steep ascents or descents, which could make a ship dangerously hard to control. On Post's previous round-the-world expedition, he had deployed a simpler solution: He instructed Gatty to move forward or back as fuel was spent, which did the trick.

Braniff's crew replaced cylinders, spark plugs, exhaust valves, and connected the fuel tanks via rubber hoses that enabled Post to switch back and forth between the 87 octane fuel he burned on take offs and the 80 octane variety he used for cruising.

The bill came to $1,763.92; but Post, to his chagrin,

only had $1,200 in the bank. The Braniff mechanics and technicians again came to his rescue, not only putting up their salaries as collateral so Post could get his plane out of the shop, but donating their off-hours to the effort. Later, as a token of his appreciation, Post made sure each worker was paid double his salary.

The *Winnie Mae* that emerged from the Braniff shop was a far better plane than the one that had entered. Yet Post knew that single-engine wooden planes like his, no matter how spruced up, were destined for obsolescence. Just that year, the Boeing 247 and Douglas DC-1, both sleek, twin-engine aircraft comprised of steel, rolled off assembly lines. The maker of the *Winnie Mae* was also moving toward all-metal construction with its Lockheed 10 Electra, which had retractable landing gear designed to cut wind drag and increase range. All of these were well beyond his budget. For this journey, the *Winnie Mae* would have to do. He prayed it would hold up.

Too antsy for a nap, Post returned to the airfield to supervise the ship's refueling, vexed by the slow pace and antiquated equipment. The airport maintenance crew in Berlin were using hand pumps—for 550 gallons of gas and 25 gallons of oil—and that, Post calculated, would add an hour to his time. This prompted the *Washington Post* to quip:

The Winnie Mae, the Winnie Mae
She flies to Berlin in a day
And then complains of the delay!

While Post waited, he dictated a dispatch to a *New York Times* reporter, which would appear under Post's byline. He recounted the "dirty weather" he faced on the journey but remarked that his "playmates"—the automatic pilot and radio transceiver—were "behaving" themselves. Two hours and 15 minutes after landing, Post climbed back in his plane with weather charts prepared by Lufthansa sticking out of his pocket.

He had planned for Novosibirsk in Siberia to be his next stop. But as he crossed the Soviet border, he couldn't find his maps for his route to Siberia, even after practically tearing apart the cabin. Worse, the line to the automatic pilot had sprung a leak, which meant he couldn't fly hands off. Frustrated, he turned back and looped down to Koenigsberg, East Prussia, sweat streaming down his face. It was the hottest day of the year, and on the ground he learned the weather had turned bad in the east. He decided to use the time to sleep. When he awoke five hours later, he faced a major decision: Should he risk flying the 3,000 miles to Novosibirsk without the automatic pilot, or stop in Moscow for repairs?

No one believed in his piloting skill more than Post did, but he was afraid he could lose his way over Siberia—the radio navigator would be useless for vast stretches, since there wouldn't be stations broadcasting, and he would have to navigate the old-fashioned way. The weather could be treacherous. Relying on maps and landmarks, it would be much harder if he had to keep his hands on the proverbial wheel. On the other hand, he would lose precious time waiting for Muscovite mechanics to effect repairs. With Siberia, the Bering Sea, and Alaska—and all of the potential hazards they offered—coming up, he couldn't afford to while away too many hours. Every minute counted.

Post went to bed almost immediately after skimming the runway in Koenigsberg, the capital of East Prussia. After a dawn wakeup call, he learned the weather between him and

Moscow was "quite bad"—heavy rain and fog, according to official reports. Post went back to sleep. By the time the weather cleared, he was so anxious to leave he roared away so fast he forgot his suitcase, and was down to the suit on his back.

Although he had commandeered the maps he needed, Koenigsberg mechanics had been unable to mend the autopilot. Post tested it anyway, and for a while thought it might be working, but faulty steering prodded him a hundred miles off course. Post went back to navigating by instrument, and the rest of the trip was uneventful until he sighted the Kremlin sparkling in the sunlight.

Meeting Wiley Post at Moscow's airport were a hundred peasants and *New York Times* reporter Walter Duranty, fresh off his Pulitzer Prize for reporting on Stalinist Russia. One of the most famous correspondents of his era, Duranty had a knack for navigating Soviet censors, since his cables had to be approved by the authorities before they would be transmitted to the U.S. Because Duranty largely relied on official sources, his 13-part prize-winning series of articles on the Soviet Union under Stalin whitewashed the atrocities that occurred. Fifty years after the fact, the *Times* would repudiate his Pulitzer, noting a "significant flaw in his coverage—his consistent underestimation of Stalin's brutality"— and that it was "completely misleading" for Duranty to take "Soviet propaganda at face value."

Because Post had not been expected in Moscow, no official was on hand to translate, so Duranty volunteered. Post told him the pipe supplying oil to the automatic pilot needed fixing, an order the *Times* reporter conveyed to the airport director. Post figured one of the rubber joints had worked loose. Perhaps his knees had knocked against the pipe, located at the bottom of the cockpit. Then Post was led to a room where a Soviet doctor examined him.

The physician felt Post's pulse, placed drops in his eye, and ordered him to lie down and sleep. Post told him he wasn't tired. He had only flown five hours and all he wanted was to refuel, get the pipe fixed, and take off again. The doctor said to lie down anyway and they'd bring dinner. Post declined. "Being hungry helps me stay awake," he explained, but to be polite, he ate a little and drank *qvass*, a pink soft drink.

According to Duranty's account, the doctor appeared "disappointed" that Post showed no signs of fatigue. "Americans of pioneer stock can do without sleep for a week," Post boasted. Duranty translated and the doctor shook his head. He told the *Times* reporter, "I have had twelve years of experience as an aviation doctor, but I never met a pilot with such steady, solid nerves and such a regular pulse after an exhausting effort and such balanced control. When I first heard he was trying to fly around the world in four or five days I thought it was madness—now I believe he will succeed."

Post went for a shave; the barber refused his tip until Post handed him some German coins and called them "keepsakes." Airport officials relayed weather updates. The forecast called for clear skies all the way to Novosibirsk, Siberia, and then cloudy beyond, with a light southeast wind. The official said radio stations in Kazan, Sverdlosk, Omsk, and Novosibirsk would call every ten minutes on a 600-meter length and give weather information in English. Post told him it wouldn't matter as long as they continually transmitted a signal for the directional finder's sake.

The last time he had been in Moscow, Post had lost valuable time because he had neglected to specify American gallons instead of imperial. This time he told airport staff not to overfill the gas tanks; otherwise he wouldn't be able to get off the ground. Mechanics mended the pipe, but the oil for it was too viscous. It had to be cut with gasoline. In the interim, Post posed for pictures and signed a customs form. "Tell him not to lose this duplicate," an official told Duranty, "because if he does the law requires he be held where he next lands."

The sun was sharp and relentless, and permeating the air was the smell of gasoline, oil, and sunflower seeds, which the Russians chewed instead of gum. Armed guards chased peasants away from the *Winnie Mae* and Post hopped in. At 5:10 p.m. he sped down the runway, over trees, and as Duranty described it, "gleaming like a seagull" he disappeared into the distance. When Post landed in Moscow, he was four hours and 24 minutes ahead of his pace from two years earlier. He left 13 hours ahead.

"I think he will do it," the airport doctor told Duranty. "I never saw such steady nerves."

The weather forecast turned out to be only partially accurate. For the first five hours, it was fine; then Post ran into the thickest clouds he had ever seen. He rose to 21,000 feet—four miles between the *Winnie Mae* and the ground—to rise on top of the ruthless haze, but the clouds climbed higher and higher, too. Post remained in the stratosphere for two hours, but the lack of oxygen made him woozy and ice formed on his wings. He descended into the fog—a dangerous tactic because he was cutting through mountain ranges.

The automatic pilot feed pipe came loose again, not that it mattered much because Post was navigating the jigsaw terrain himself. The undercarriage of the *Winnie Mae* scraped a hillside that suddenly popped up through the mist. It so unnerved him Post considered putting on his parachute.

Post knew how fragile life was; it could turn in the instant it took a sledgehammer to strike a spike and a steel fragment to pierce his eye. During his wing walker days, he had made it a habit to tempt death—pulling his ripcord at the last possible second to see how far he could fall, basking in the adulation of the bloodthirsty crowd. To conserve fuel, he had often let the tank run dry, which stalled the engine. Only then would he switch tanks to reignite the propeller, relishing how much it scared passengers. It became part of his practical joke repertoire. Now, though, he was all business, knowing full well he was one ill-conceived decision away from crashing and burning.

He kept his eye trained on the altimeter and compass, and whenever he faced a rough stretch he talked to himself. "You've got to get through somehow." His wife, "Mae, and those boys in Oklahoma"—the men who financed this journey—"are counting on me." Post floated down to a more manageable altitude, and for six hours flew blind by "dead reckoning," aided sporadically by radio messages from Sverdlovsk. Eventually he found himself 200 feet off the ground, following the tracks of the Trans-Siberian railway until they spidered off in different directions.

Lost again, Post landed in a field. Before long two peasants rode by in a horse-driven cart. Through hand gestures and mangling the pronunciation of Novosibirsk, Post finally made them understand where he wanted to go. The two men pointed in opposite directions: One claimed Novosibirsk was 180 miles to the west; the other 840 miles east. They eventually agreed Novosibirsk was east, but couldn't say how far. Post landed a second time near Tartarsk and shortly after picked up Novosibirsk's radio signal, which enabled him to fix his position. Even then he floundered in the mist and almost missed the airport. An Associated Press reporter was speaking to Novosibirsk Airport officials by telephone when Post alighted. "We're expecting him any minute," began the attendant. "Just a second—he's coming down now."

Waiting in the wings was Fay Gillis, a 24-year-old American aviatrix living in Moscow with her parents, both engineers at a zinc factory. Post had met her in 1931 after his record-setting trek with Gatty, while she was on an extended visit to the U.S. He had enlisted her help in organizing logistics. In a telegram to her, he wrote:

YOU ARRIVE NOVOSIBIRSK BY JULY FIRST STOP ARRANGE GAS PLANES IN TWO HOURS WHILE I SLEEP STOP THEN FLY WITH ME TO KHABAROVSK TO DIRECT SERVICE THERE STOP GET ME BEST MAPS NOVOSIBIRSK-KHABAROVSK STOP WILL PAY YOUR EXPENSES STOP REGARDS WILEY POST.

The first time Gillis went up in an airplane, the tail came apart and she and her instructor were forced to bail. That made her the first female member of the Caterpillar Club, comprised of pilots forced to parachute out of a plane to save their lives. She had learned to fly when she was just

19, spoke fluent Russian, and was an original founder of the "Ninety Nines," a woman's pilot organization. (Amelia Earhart served as the group's first president.) For the three years prior to working for Post, she was a correspondent in Russia, covering aviation activities for the *New York Herald Tribune*, and a special reporter for *The New York Times* and the Associated Press. She was also the first American woman to fly a Soviet civil airplane and the first foreigner to own a Soviet glider.

Gillis liked to say she became a journalist in self-defense. In the Stalinist Soviet Union, dilettantes were not tolerated, and all Russian women, from the president's wife on down, worked. As an expatriate she met a number of journalists, including the *Times'* Duranty. He and the others lived such fascinating lives, visited so many places, and did such outlandish things without batting an eyelash that Gillis decided it was an ideal career. In Moscow she quickly learned how to write around censorship—to tell a censorable story in uncensorable terms.

After hitching a ride in the back of a mail plane from Moscow, tucked between bails of correspondence, Gillis had been in Novosibirsk for three weeks. In that time, she had gathered two tons of gasoline and a half a ton of oil, more than enough to slake the *Winnie Mae*'s thirst. She made sure the landing field was mowed every other day and that qualified mechanics were on hand, collected maps prepared especially for Post by civil aviation authorities in Moscow, and arranged for a special room so he could rest while his ship was refueled. "I am saving my last piece of American soap for him, which he ought to appreciate," she said.

The conditions were primitive—Gillis' hotel didn't have

hot water, so she took a bath at a local factory—but she was excited by the prospect of assisting on a historic flight. She also plotted her first major scoop for *The New York Herald Tribune*. Originally, as the telegram shows, Post had wanted Gillis to ride with him to Khabarovsk. "Wiley did not tell me where he was going to put me, but I would straddle the tail of the plane, if necessary, to go along with him," she said. That, however, would have jeopardized the solo standing of his flight. Instead, Post promised her a ride in New York—a chit she promised to cash in one day.

While Post reclined on a couch at the airport, Gillis fed him bouillon and fruit and learned he had an exclusive contract with *The New York Times*. Gillis was forced to scoop her own scoop—The Trib was the *Times*' biggest competitor—taking down Post's dispatch and then transmitting it for him. She then filed her own story. Once it was cleared, she sweetly asked the operator not to put through any more calls, and the line between Novosibirsk and Moscow went dead for the rest of the night. The other reporters were livid, but Gillis didn't care. She had her scoop. (Two years later Gillis eloped to Ethiopia to cover the war with Linton Wells, the swashbuckling correspondent who once held the record for traveling the world by plane, train, automobile, and steamer. In 1936, the couple took with them a leopard, lioness and a cheetah to Hollywood, where the leopard often accompanied Gillis on interviews. After that, she was named one of the first female White House correspondents.)

Post stayed in Novosibirsk long enough for his plane to take on fuel and then pushed on to Irkutsk, where there were better repair facilities. He found out Koenigsberg aviation officials wanted to transport his suitcase on a commercial plane, but Post said, "I can't wait for it. Just have it sent home for me." He was not proud of his performance thus far. "I hoped to be at Irkutsk by this time," he said, "but I have still got a chance to beat our record, and I am out to do it." But the strain of all that dead weather flying was taking its toll.

Halfway around the world in Big Spring, Texas, D.J. Laine hung near a newspaper office, awaiting reports of his famous son-in-law's progress. "How's iron man getting along?" he asked. Laine, a cotton farmer, laughed when told the robot pilot was tired but Post was not. In an editorial, the *Washington Post* lauded Post's legendary ability to stay awake. "The chief marvel of Wiley Post's spectacular flight around the top of the world is not the endurance of the machine, but the endurance of the man." But, it warned, "the most dangerous stretch of Post's route lies between Khabarovsk and Nome. The Sea of Okhotsk, Kamchatka and Bering Sea are rarely clear of storms and fog."

The truth was, Post was dead tired. Gillis could see the fatigue etched in his face, and he had almost half a world to go. A tired pilot made mistakes, and unless he could get that autopilot repaired in Irkutsk, Post could find himself facing split second decisions—a jutting mountaintop peeking through clouds directly in his path, faulty instruments and mechanical breakdowns, stormy weather.

Any one of them alone could spell disaster.

CHAPTER 8

Arctic Wasteland

JIMMIE MATTERN CRIED A LOT THE FIRST TWO DAYS HE was marooned. His ship was crushed and broken, and he was 100 miles into the Arctic Circle with only three chocolate bars and the clothes on his back. He axed a hole in the fuselage to create a makeshift bed, lining the walls with paper maps to help insulate against the cold, and jerry-rigged a cook stove/heater from a fuel container and engine cylinder. He also had a gun, which had been hidden in a secret compartment built into the ship for emergencies just like this. On his wrist was a top-of-the-line Wittnauer watch—the company helped sponsor his trip, and the watch was the one thing that kept ticking after the crash. To give himself something to do, Mattern kept a journal. Someday explorers might find him, and he wanted them to know what kind of man he was.

The landscape was bleak, his prospects bleaker. Each day Mattern dragged his injured ankle behind him to the river and prayed a boat would pass, and each night he trekked back to his ship. Bruised and sore from his improvised landing, he also developed blisters on his feet from his river walks. It was worst around midnight, when temperatures dipped into the 20s.

He was fortunate he had crashed during summer. If it had been autumn, he might already be dead of exposure. His leather flight suit was a godsend. But his makeshift heater caused problems—there was no ventilation in the back of the plane, and it filled up with smoke. As a result, he was cold much of the night.

On his third day Mattern shot a duck. It wasn't easy. The animals of the tundra steered clear of him, as if they intuited his desperate intentions. He stashed it in the river to keep it cold, complimenting himself for his foresight in bringing salt. Tomorrow he would feast—just as soon as he finished constructing a raft out of pieces of driftwood fastened with bailing wire. He rigged an American flag on a pole ready to stick in the front. Anadyr, an outpost, was within 100 miles, if his calculations were correct. If he followed the river, Mattern figured he could be there in four days, perhaps five, depending on the current, unless he came upon a settlement along the way.

After another frigid night in his plane's carcass, he gathered a piece of iron from the *Century of Progress'* tail on which to put the duck to roast and limped to the river. He was heartbroken to discover that seagulls had poached his duck; scattered bones and feathers were all that remained. Hovering above, the seagulls taunted him. Mattern imagined them saying, "Die, will you?" Glassy and weak from hunger, he was afraid he was losing his mind. No rational man would have left a dead duck in a stream assuming it would be there the next morning. His eyes stung from the glare of ice and snow and his feet were wet. Mattern moped to his raft, which he had tied to some weeds. It had almost floated away with the tide. He pulled it to shore. At six in the evening he returned to the *Century of Progress*. He had fire and some tea, but nothing to boil water in. This made him angry until he noticed the wind howling. A storm was brewing.

It rained all night and day. Mattern remained in his ship, listening to the percussive drops. He caught a glimpse of himself in a mirror. The ghost that stared back was gaunt, hair a cubist mess, skin rougher than the leather on his flight suit, a bristly beard and grime etching his face. The eyes weren't those of a pilot anymore. They were of a man who might not be long of this earth.

Alaskan bush pilot Joe Crosson had once told him to stay with his ship if he crashed, but Mattern was 600 miles from Nome. His were different circumstances. Although he was sure pilots would be searching for him, the land was so vast and remote there was little chance they would find him. He studied a map and estimated he'd need to float 80 to 100 miles down river. Figure 20 miles a day and he could be in Anadyr in five days, God willing. In the wreckage Mattern picked out a bag of cookie crumbs. There was one large piece and several smaller ones, which he ate slowly. That would be his three meals for the day.

All this time alone gave Mattern time for reflection. He wrote in his diary: *I have been thinking about a lot of things lately. I pray every day. I think of my mother and hope that she is not worrying so much that it would affect her health. I, of course, think of so many things. I could have done better with my life. I have always tried to do what is right. I did want to make money. Well, now I realize how useless money is and of no value in the Arctic wastes of Siberia. I have over one hundred dollars in my pocket, and it won't even make fire to keep me warm… I would have given anything for a smooth field instead of money.* A field suitable for landing would have been worth everything—he could have fixed his oil line problem and taken off again. Then this whole nightmare would have only been a slight inconvenience adding a few hours to his time. *But the breaks seemed against me on the flight from the start. My only hope is to get out of here and back to civilization. That's all I want. My foolish days of records is over and I want to settle down to a quiet life.*

The more he wrote, the more tired he felt. A wet fog draped over the ship, the air thick and cold. Mattern left his ship to go hunting, his ankles weak and uncertain, his feet cold, wet, and numb. He wasn't able to bag anything; the little food he had left—half a chocolate bar, some cookie crumbs—had almost run out. By the river, he lit a fire with green bushes, which smoked and smoldered, hoping someone would see it from the air or heading down the river: a fur trader, an Eskimo, anybody. No one came. Mattern made up his mind. He would take his chances on the raft.

But the heavens wept icy rain, and Mattern holed up in his plane for the night. The next morning he penned a note, which he left inside the fractured fuselage of the *Century of Progress*. He explained how he had crashed, was almost out of food, and gave his best guess as to his coordinates: latitude 64:35 west and longitude 175:30 north. *I have made a raft and am going down the river,* he wrote. *If you locate the airplane and I have not been found, I will be between here and a hundred miles down stream. I will stay to the right bank out of the wind going down... I have a map and a compass so to establish landmarks as I go along. Keep looking, boys, as I want to get out of this mess. I will never give up. Will be looking for you.* Mattern signed and dated the note.

The weather was gorgeous, warmer than it had been. Mattern made two trips to the raft, one with a cylinder from his Wasp engine, the other with maps and his flying suit, carrying his gun both directions. Weak and starving, he fell several times, hardly able to get back on his feet.

He loaded the raft. After saying a prayer, he pushed it into the stream.

It sank.

Mattern jumped into the glacier-cold water to save the cylinder and maps, battling the current so he could drag everything back to shore. Soaked and shivering, he needed to build a fire right away, a big one. He tried to burn the whole beach down. In the process, fuel that soaked his clothes when he had crashed caught fire. The pain was searing. Panicking, he staggered into the river. When he emerged he had several burn marks. He crouched next to the fire to dry off. The skin where he was burnt stung and his teeth ached. *I am now very discouraged and don't know how things will turn out,* he wrote. Mattern finally fell into a dream, warm for the first time since he'd crashed.

There were times during his Arctic incarceration when he felt like giving up. The lack of food and human companionship made it hard to cope. He found the constant silence unnerving. Usually decisive, he couldn't make up his mind. *I have kept the fire going all day and just been looking for a boat,* he wrote. *I don't know whether to start walking or not. Really don't think I should. I would get weak and then if the airplane was located I would not be found. Yesterday I shot a muskrat and ate him. It made me sick but filled my stomach.*

Halfway around the world, a month's worth of American newspaper headlines told Mattern's tale of trepidation and dashed hopes:

MATTERN IS ALOFT ON DANGEROUS HOP; TEXAN OFF FOR NOME FROM SIBERIA IN SPITE OF OVERCAST SKIES (*Washington Post*)

LONE WORLD FLYER OVERDUE IN ALASKA; FEARED VICTIM OF FOG (*Chicago Tribune*)

MATTERN MISSING ON ALASKA FLIGHT: BAD WEATHER ON ROUTE FOR AND NEAR-FREEZING TEMPERATURE CAUSE ALARM AS FUEL TIME LIMIT PASSES (*New York Times*)

FISHING VESSELS ON LOOKOUT FOR WORLD AIRMAN; FOGS IN BERING SEA HIDE FATE OF JIMMIE MATTERN (*Washington Post*)

NAVY SENT IN SEARCH OF MATTERN; ALL SHIPS IN VICINITY ORDERED TO HUNT FOR LOST WORLD FLYER (*Los Angeles Times*)

NO WORD IS RECEIVED (*New York Times*)

MATTERN SEARCH HELD UP BY FOG
(*Chicago Tribune*)

MATTERN REMAINS UNREPORTED
(*Hartford Courant*)

JAPAN KEEPS UP HUNT FOR MATTERN
(*New York Times*)

MATTERN HUNT PARTY FORMED; REWARD
OF $5000 OFFERED (*Los Angeles Times*)

STORMS HALT PLANE ON WAY TO HUNT
FOR MATTERN (*Chicago Tribune*)

RUSSIANS SEEK MATTERN; SEARCH TO BE
INTENSIFIED (*New York Times*)

Mattern camped by the river in the event a boat floated by, but was running out of wood—he'd picked clean the entire area. On his way to the plane for more gasoline, he hobbled up a hill for a view of the surrounding area. His heart crashed when all he could see for miles and miles was unyielding arctic waste. The unvarnished sun also meant something else. He slapped his arm. Mosquitoes. By morning, he was swarmed.

He worked on another raft while waist-deep in water. To be sure it would float, he tested it out wearing just his underwear. Then he put on his clothes, piled his few belongings onboard, and rode it face down, paddling with his hands with icy water breaking over his head. For several hours he kept at it, until a strong current pushed him back the way he had come. The tide must have come in from the Anadyr Gulf, and in no time he was back to a small island directly across the river from his makeshift camp.

Ten days into his primitive incarceration, and Mattern was right back where he had started. He tried not to allow himself to think it was hopeless, but a shadow crossed his face. Looking up, he saw vultures circling. *Waiting for me to die*, he thought.

On the island, he came across a breeding ground for ducks, eggs scattered everywhere. While most of the shells were empty, a few were ready to hatch. He left them in the sun to incubate, but the weather was about to get dreary, judging by clouds sweeping across the sky. Mattern was wet, starting to shiver. He built a fire. *I must have looked funny carrying big logs up the beach, for the raft, in my underwear with a glacier in the background and a beard of two weeks*, he scribbled in his diary. He tried grass as kindling, but it wouldn't catch. *Always something wrong*, he thought, but the armfuls of hay he collected did burn. What's more, it smoked, which kept the mosquitoes at bay.

Two specks in the distance caught his eye—so far away he couldn't make out what they were. Mattern directed his compass on them and went away for a few minutes. When he returned, the specks had moved. *Oh God, I hope it is what I think it is*. He watched for what seemed an eternity, but the specks remained cemented in the same position. His disappointment cut deep. He figured he had been hallucinating.

The sky opened up just enough so that a ray of sun shone down. Mattern could see oars striking water. They were coming straight toward him. *Yes! Yes! They really are boats. They are moving slowly toward me. I screamed as loud as I could. Oh, boy, what a feeling. I am saved!"*

Several minutes later it was actually two boats that pulled up to shore, holding Eskimos. In the larger vessel were three men in furs, accompanied by a woman, two teenage girls, a five-year-old boy, and two sled dogs. In the other were two adolescent boys rowing a man, a woman, and three small children.

Mattern looked at them. They looked at him. A couple of grunts, but nobody said a word. Then Mattern, after grabbing a few threadbare possessions, piled in.

Mattern thought they were Eskimos, but they were, in fact, an indigenous people who had come to Siberia after the Eskimos. The Russians called them Chukchi, and they were the largest Native nation (about 15,000) on the Asian side of the North Pacific. The word Chukchi was derived from *Chauchu*, a Chukchi word meaning "rich in reindeer."

Not long after Mattern settled into the primitive boat, two ducks floated downstream. One of the Chukchi perfectly imitated their quack and the ducks turned toward the boat, at which point another Chukchi shot them. After scooping the carcasses out of the water, on they went. Mattern had practically starved for weeks because he couldn't catch a duck, yet in 30 minutes his new travel mates had bagged two.

Mattern wrote, *The Eskimos never stop rowing. How strong they are. They are all dressed in raw furs, the out side of a fox turned inside. The mother is nursing the baby. The boys play with it. They seem very affectionate. The mother makes a noise like a rattlesnake to keep the baby quiet. The dogs sleep all the time. The girls seem bashful. It has started to get cold. I put on my flying suit. You should see them watch me use those zippers. It was wonderful to them, you could tell.*

They offered Mattern baked bread, which tasted glorious, especially after the half-raw muskrat he'd eaten. He tried to communicate his thanks with hand gestures and by drawing, but nothing registered. They communicated with grunts, which to Mattern's ear sounded like strings of "ahs" and "uhs."

With the sun pumping rays and light 22 hours a day, the two teenaged boys paddled until they found a place to pitch camp, spread bearskins on the ground, and prepare meals. Mattern watched as the group went about their chores. The men trudged out to the tundra looking for geese, while the teenaged boys pitched the tents and the women built a fire and prepared biscuit dough from flour and river water. Then the women picked herbs and roots—things that could have kept Mattern alive if he had known what to look for.

His hands were clenched in a ball and his teeth were loose and achy. Lack of nourishment had caused Mattern to come down with scurvy. A woman handed him thyme boiled in water and indicated that he should swallow it— hours later he was cured. The children ran up and down the beach and played in the snow. The men returned with two of the fattest geese Mattern had ever seen, their throats tied together and draped around one of the men's necks, and the women scooped bear fat out of half a five-gallon fuel can and fried the biscuit dough.

They all sat around a table on their haunches and supped

on biscuits and honey and drank tea, Mattern's first real food in weeks. Then everyone pitched in to carry the hundred or so fox and bearskins from the boat to store on high land.

Mattern learned they were actually three families of Eskimos, the only humans passing through these parts. They maintained a trap line 200 miles long, where they collected game, honey, and furs. Once a year they traveled down this river with their furs to trade for flour, guns, and ammunition. They were on their way home when they came upon Mattern. As unlucky as he had been, he was lucky he had run into them; otherwise, he would have never gotten out. *The Eskimos didn't know that I hadn't eaten. The Eskimos didn't really know what I was all about. They just wondered where I came from, I guess. They had never seen anything like me and the way I was dressed... As I am writing this, they are looking over my shoulder. They have never seen anyone write.*

He produced his map kit and offered two of the boys pliers and another a hunting knife. One was enamored with his Pratt & Whitney tool kit, and Mattern gave that away, too. Each gift was received as a miracle, and Mattern was happy he could return, in some small way, the generosity their families were extending to him. *As I sit here now by a warm fire, all the little Eskimos are playing in the snow, there are tents to sleep in and a hundred bear and fox furs to get under and protect me from the coldest place on earth: Arctic Siberia. I feel that God has been great to me... My only thoughts of sorrow are my wonderful airplane put to sleep on the frozen tundra north forever.* He had migrated from the crushed shell of the *Century of Progress* to a land that time had forgotten.

It took four days and nights before they reached a settlement, marked by caribou hide tents 15 feet in diameter.

The Chukchi were soon at work on their side of the river, fishing for salmon. They carved out the bellies and tossed them in a barrel while hanging the rest of the fish in strips to dry. For a pastime the Chukchi played checkers on a bag with scratches on it, using rocks and wadded up paper as pieces. Mattern slept peacefully in the tent that night under furs, a fire going in the middle with smoke drawing through a small hole at the top.

The next day he was paddled across the river to meet the tribal chief, who invited Mattern to stay in his tent. *They are amazed at seeing me, a white man, dressed in a tanned leather zippered flying suit. They gather around as if I were a sideshow attraction. As a matter of fact I am just that. Everyone wants to come to the tent to look at me. If I fall asleep the Eskimo squaws wake me up zipping my flight suit.*

As he waited day after day for a boat to take him to Anadyr, he tried to blend in as much as possible. That night the Chukchi celebrated the capture of a herd of caribou. After slaughtering one, they danced around a fire for eight hours, shouting "Hoyt! Hoyt! Hoyt!" Mattern joined in with their Thanksgiving cry, which to him sounded like "Wa Wa Ah Woop." The tribe paid homage because their existence largely depended on the caribou. Their clothes and tents were made with it, the dog sleds were tied together with the raw hide, and it was a source of food. No part was unused.

To these Siberian tribesmen, America was like heaven, and they looked at Mattern as if he wasn't of this world. Outside of the animals and fish, herbs, and tundra, most everything that made their lives easier originated from that mystical place called "America." It was stamped on the crates that held guns, ammunition, flour, rope, traps, and fishing equipment. For centuries before the Russian Revolution, which had occurred just 15 years earlier, there had been continuous barter between Nome, Alaska and Anadyr, Siberia. Nothing of quality was labeled "Russia." It all came from America.

The next morning, Mattern crossed the river to visit the families that had rescued him. When he got there, they were gone. Through pantomime he learned they were traveling to Anadyr, and Mattern grew frantic. No matter how hard he tried, he couldn't get his point across. Finally he pulled out the $100 in cash he had. That they understood. Within a few hours he was bound for Anadyr. *I am writing this in the boat with six Eskimos. Three rowing, two others and myself in the middle and a very old one steering in the rear with his cape up over his head and the sun setting at his back. What a great feeling to again be moving and what a great picture. The land has sloped gradually to the shore and snow is along the beach with a pink sky, a smooth lake and a boat full of very picaresque people. Every stroke of the oars says, 'AMERICA.'*

They reached a lake and put up a sail, the wind pushing them onward. Several hours later they stopped for tea and biscuits until a motorboat pulled in further up the beach. Mattern walked up the shoreline to meet it and indicated what he wanted. A few hours later he arrived in Anadyr, 70 miles north of the Arctic Circle, where Mattern spoke English to another human being for the first time in more than a month. They discussed plans for salvaging Mattern's plane—horses, tools, men, and a barge. After Mattern took a bath and ate canned beef and beans, which tasted heavenly, he went to the telegraph office.

His message consisted of six words: *Safe at Anadyr, Siberia. Jimmie Mattern.*

CHAPTER 9

Flat

WILEY POST MOTORED OVER SIBERIA'S EASTERN seaboard and turned up to the Arctic Circle, cutting through the same mountain range as Mattern had before he tumbled out of the sky. The difference was that Post encountered far worse weather. He flew blind for seven hours without the autopilot; a preordained course based on unreliable maps would have been suicide. Instead he relied on his compass, calculating drift from the way clouds swirled around mountain peaks—practically the only land he would see.

Piloting a plane for 1800 miles is challenging to a rested pilot, but Post hadn't slept since Moscow. He picked up radio transmissions from WAMCATS—the Washington-Alaska

Military Cable and Telegraph System in Nome, Teller and Hot Springs, Alaska—while making his way over the Bering Strait. Zeroing in on the signals, he was able to navigate with almost no visibility. When mountains appeared above the clouds, he knew he had hit Alaska. Maneuvering to the north side of the mountains where the wind had puffed the clouds away, Post dropped low and edged back toward the coast, following the shoreline around Cape Prince of Wales to Nome, where he buzzed the radio station and airport.

Instead of stopping in Nome to refuel, pick up fresh weather reports, and rest, Post decided to keep going to Fairbanks. Although he was dog-tired and far ahead of his 1931 time, he felt a tremendous urge to press on. He had heard Jimmie Mattern was not only alive, but might be able to return to the air and be on his way to Nome. Post didn't have a minute to spare. He surveyed the radio chatter and realized it wasn't simply man versus machine or man versus nature anymore. It was once again man versus man. Although Mattern's achievement would always carry an asterisk, newspaper and radio reporters had once again begun framing it as a race, and in the minds of the public that was the shape it had taken.

Not soon after, Post flew into thick fog and his automatic direction finder quit. Although the radio stations continued to broadcast, he wasn't receiving any signals. He climbed over the clouds, expecting to pick up Fairbanks, but all he got was static. Wandering all over the interior of Alaska, dodging mountains, including 20,000-foot Mt. McKinley, and following rivers that led nowhere, he was completely lost.

Noel Wien, a well-known Alaskan bush pilot, and his

wife Ada were in a Bellanca also on the way to Fairbanks when they spotted the *Winnie Mae*. They were aware that Wiley Post was flying around the globe, yet here he was circling over forestland. They tired to radio him with directions to Fairbanks, but Post didn't respond nor did he see them. Their Bellanca couldn't keep pace with Post's Lockheed, so they continued to Fairbanks, expecting to see Post there. When he wasn't, they wondered if the One-Eyed Wonder had put his plane in a circling pattern so he could nap. Seven hours after arriving over Nome, barely able to keep his eye open and fuel running low, Post looked for a place—any place—to land.

Below was a tiny village with a very short, primitive airstrip. When he saw the wireless masts, he decided to come down at all costs and find out where he was. At least he wouldn't be completely cut off from civilization. When Post swooped down for a closer look, he estimated that the uneven, pockmarked runway was perhaps 700 feet long, punctuated with a ditch at the far end. He wouldn't be able to use his brakes; the strip was too bumpy. Actually there really wasn't enough real estate for him to safely land, but he was desperate. He had been in the air for 22 hours and 42 minutes, and hadn't had a wink of sleep in close to 40 hours.

At 3:30 p.m. local time, Post brought the *Winnie Mae* down, greeting the runway's edge. The wheels bounded over the unpaved surface and the plane jounced and swerved. Without warning, the right landing gear support collapsed. The plane's nose pitched forward and the propeller dug into the ground. The ship tipped up in the air, her tail pointing straight up while her nose looked straight down. Miraculously, Post was unhurt.

The mine manager scurried over to help him out of the wreckage. Recognizing the famous Wiley Post on a record-setting mission, he asked if the *Winnie Mae* could be repaired.

Post didn't know. He was 1000 miles from nowhere with a ship that wouldn't fly, hobbled by a busted propeller and splintered landing gear. Post was angry with himself for not stopping in Nome to rest and pick up fresh weather reports. If Gatty had been with him, this accident would have never happened. But Post had been impatient, and now he was paying for it.

The miner led the exhausted pilot to a shack.

Post, almost too tired to care, curled up on a cot and passed out.

CHAPTER 10

Trapped

FROM ANADYR, JIMMIE MATTERN TRAVELED BY MOTOR-ized barge back up the river, past the Eskimo camp, and over to the crash site to salvage his plane's instrument board, propeller, and Wasp engine. Accompanied by a score of Eskimos and two dog sled teams, he visited the grass hut he had lined with maps to keep the wind out. Mattern collected the maps for Anadyr to Edmonton, thinking he could continue his journey and still be the first man to fly around the world solo. All he had to do was salvage the remains of the Vega, get to Nome, and locate another ship he could pilot to New York. After what he had been through, this didn't seem implausible.

He chopped the motor off the wooden frame with an

axe—it fell on its nose into the snow. The two dog sleds were connected by a makeshift platform, and the men, straining under the weight, placed the engine on top. Six ropes and three men to a rope, pulling like mad and bent close to the ground, with the dogs champing at their bits. But the motor was so heavy they could only pull it a few feet at a time. Mattern and his Russian interpreter walked the 30 minutes from the plane to the river to wait. When the equipment was loaded onto the barge, they took off downstream until they got to the Eskimo settlement.

While they waited for the tide to change, Mattern took his interpreter with him so he could explain who he was and how he had come to stay with them. Mattern found the reception to his story exciting. *They'll be talking about this up here for a long time*, he thought. Then they sailed the rest of the way to Anadyr, where he boxed up the remains of his ship and had it sent to the U.S.

Mattern spent days cooling his heels, waiting for an exit visa from Soviet authorities. But officials wouldn't give him permission to depart for Nome. After several days he learned one of Russia's top pilots, Sigismund Levanevsky, was on his way from the Black Sea to pick him up. The U.S. didn't recognize Stalin's Soviet Union, which was vying for international respectability, and now Mattern had become a pawn between two unfriendly nations. That meant his rescue could take several more days, if not weeks. He telegraphed his manager in New York, who set about searching for another plane so that Mattern could take a plucky last lap in an interrupted solo round-the-world flight.

Help came from an unexpected source: a Brooklyn brewer whom Mattern had never met. A group of Mattern's friends at Floyd Bennett Field were determined to locate a plane for him. While seeking funds, which were in short supply during those downtrodden economic times, Irving Friedman, president of Brooklyn's Kings Brewery, entered their lives. Friedman was not particularly interested in aviation, but Mattern's friends "sounded so sincere" he donated money to buy the sturdy ship that Clyde Pangborn had flown over the Pacific.

The rescue party, led by pilots William Alexander and Fred Fetterman, set out for Alaska in the hopes they could then leave for Siberia. But an American plane required Soviet permission to land, while Levanevsky was going to need permission from the U.S. to touch down in Alaska. Moscow and Washington were not, however, on speaking terms.

Friedman exchanged his brewer's cap for that of a diplomat and took on the role of intermediary, and messages from both sides were exchanged through him. Struggling with hard-to-pronounce Russian names, Friedman accepted cablegrams from an unofficial Soviet representative in Washington and passed them to the U.S. State Department, and then carried the official replies to the unofficial Russian. It took a fair amount of diplomatic wrangling before the two countries reached a deal that allowed Levanevsky to land in Nome, where Friedman's rescue plane would be waiting for Mattern.

Back in Anadyr, when a reporter for Russia's state-run media asked Mattern whether he would allow Levanevsky to fly him to Alaska, he proposed a different plan. "Yes, I will," Mattern answered, "but that would mean a thousand extra miles of flying over water for me to return to Anadyr in an

American plane, and then to complete my solo flight from [there]." Mattern said he would prefer for the Soviets to allow two friends of his to fly a plane from Alaska to Siberia so that Mattern could fly it solo back to the U.S., while Levanevsky transported the American pilots to Alaska. That way American and Russian pilots would be working together in a spirit of cooperation. The Russians ignored Mattern's request, and he killed time by taking Russian language lessons, learned how to play "Home Sweet Home" on the balalaika, and filed stories of his adventures to *The New York Times*, which held exclusive rights.

Levanevsky's plane was delayed by bad weather, and Mattern became increasingly agitated. Then he received a devastating message from Nome: Wiley Post was in Siberia, making great time on his way around the world. His one-eyed rival was in Irkutsk, about to leave for Khabarovsk, a city on the east coast of Russia. To think that Mattern had a Wasp Lockheed, pontoon-equipped, sitting only three and a half hours flying time from where he was. Russian bureaucracy was making his blood boil. He couldn't help himself. He knew he was lucky to be alive, but he was having trouble containing his desire to get back into the race.

No use griping, though. If he couldn't have the record, Mattern figured he might as well assist his rival in some small way. It was the sporting thing to do. Having flown these parts, he knew the weather could be a back-breaker. Mattern made his way to the Anadyr wireless station and put his basic Russian to good use. He helped the operators, who spoke next to no English, translate their weather reports, which were then forwarded to the United States Signal Corps through its station at Nome. Judging by the chatter over the radio, Post was practically right overhead. Then Mattern returned to his room for a nap. He woke up an hour later to the drone of a plane engine. Mattern put on his boots and raced outside.

A spacious two-engine airplane with pontoons circled the town, headed across the bay, returned, and circled overhead again. Mattern could tell the pilot was careful—he was taking a thorough look before landing. The water was choppy in the middle of the bay, so the pilot brought the ship down close to the beach and taxied to a boat dock next to the shop owned by Mattern's interpreter.

Mattern went to greet Commander Levanevsky, a lithe, taciturn Soviet war hero and a favorite of Josef Stalin's. He had just completed a harrowing five-day journey, flying from Far Eastern Siberia, skirting Imperial Japan and up and over the Pacific to the Arctic Circle and Anadyr. Along the way he rode into a sheet of fog thick enough that it forced him to skim the Pacific so low waves lashed his wingtips. He landed near Okhotsk for the night.

The next morning the fog lifted, and Levanevsky ran into a hurricane with winds upwards of 120 mph and visibility of just a few feet. He narrowly missed a cliff. Subsequent stages, including a detour over the aptly named Isle of Confusion, were not much better. A trip that would normally take a day in clear weather ended up taking five times as long.

Levanevsky didn't speak English, but brought a bottle of whiskey and indicated Mattern should join him and his small crew. The Russians lived up to their reputations, and after five hours of hand waving and shouting around a table, Mattern stumbled back to his room. As he passed out on his bunk, Mattern wondered how Post was doing. He figured

Wiley was either right on his tail or perhaps a little ahead. But with a trip like this, lots could go wrong. Even if Post got to Alaska first, that didn't ensure victory.

Mattern vowed that just as soon as the room stopped spinning, he and the Russians would leave for Nome.

The race was back on.

The next morning, after a Soviet supply ship transferred fuel to Levanevsky's seaplane, a twin-motored Dornier Wal, which sported a four-bladed propeller in the front and double-bladed propeller in the rear. The interior was so spacious Mattern could practically jog from the cockpit to the tail without ducking. The crew ran into trouble with the oil when mosquitoes clogged the funnel, which had to be rinsed every few minutes. Practically the whole town came to see them off. Mattern was excited to leave Anadyr, a place that had gone from his salvation to virtual prison.

Levanevsky taxied to the center of the river and opened the throttle, the propellers spinning madly and the overloaded plane floating over the water. A hundred yards later, Mattern knew they wouldn't get off the ground. There was simply too much weight onboard. In addition to gear, fuel, and plane, approximately 1200 pounds of man, including Levanevsky, a pilot, co-pilot, two mechanics, and Mattern, kept the plane on earth. Nevertheless, Levanevsky tried again, with similar results. The Russian pilot was faced with a choice: Leave one of his compatriots in Anadyr while he chauffeured Mattern to Alaska, or cut back on fuel. He opted to dump100 gallons of gasoline weighing about 600 pounds overboard. After a few more tries the mammoth flying boat staggered into the air.

The weather was sunshiney and clear, and at 5:30 p.m.,

they crossed the Russian breakwater and headed toward the easternmost piece of Russian territory. Before they got there, however, a shroud of fog descended over the water. Levanevsky pushed the plane up 2000 feet and changed course for St. Lawrence Island for the final 125-mile leg to Nome. Two layers of clouds melded together, however, and Levanevsky, lacking the equipment to fly blind with which Mattern had equipped the *Century of Progress*, turned back to St. Lawrence Island, where they landed on a remote each to camp for the night.

Mattern was antsy being so close to American soil and was becoming fatalistic. He wondered what else would go wrong. He got his answer the next day, after resting until noon while waiting for the sun to burn away the fog. Unable to understand Russian patter, Mattern surmised that Levanevsky had dumped too much fuel and didn't have enough to get to Nome. The nearest land was more than a hundred miles hence. Fingers crossed, they took off. To conserve fuel, Levanevsky hugged the water, surfing over the waves. More ten-ply fog descended and the Russian pilot struggled with visibility. Mattern strolled back through the ship to check the gas gauges. They had about five minutes of gasoline left with no land in sight.

The idea of sitting in the Bering Sea for two weeks stabbed Mattern's heart. Luckily, three minutes before the engine quit, Levanevsky spotted land. He curved sharply down the beach until sighting a small city. That's when the motor quit, and the ship came down with a splash on its pontoons. They were four miles from Nome. Mattern almost had to be restrained from jumping into the water and swimming the last bit. Levanevsky ordered a rubber lifeboat inflated and Mattern joined him to go ashore, leaving several crew aboard.

Walking down the beach, they sighted several launches coming from Nome. The tug *Genevieve* picked them up and returned the two pilots back to the plane, which was towed to the Lomen Company docks, where Mattern was greeted as a conquering hero. He noticed several familiar faces from his time working as an Alaskan bush pilot. Stepping on American soil was the happiest moment of his trip.

In Nome, Bob Ellis, an Alaskan bush pilot, welcomed Mattern to America. So did a couple of journalists, who informed Mattern of Post's crash in Flat. Mattern said all the right things: "I am sorry he suffered misfortune," and offered to aid his fallen rival. What he really wanted was to grab a plane and shoot back to New York. He figured it would take two days.

But Ellis had bad news. The Bellanca the Brooklyn brewer purchased crashed en route—in Hazelton, British Columbia, near Prince Rupert. Mattern would have to pick it up there, but Ellis wouldn't take off from Nome until the same weather that had vexed Post cleared. Ellis had survived this long because he didn't fool with tempestuous weather. In the meantime, Mattern purchased gold rings for Levanevsky and his crew, and in sign of respect, he and Ellis flew several miles out over the Bering Sea to accompany the Soviet ship on its way back home.

CHAPTER 11

Help from a Faithful Friend

ONLY 230 MILES FROM NOME, WILEY POST AWOKE from a hard nap to find his beloved *Winnie Mae* mounted on a wooden derrick. The miner who greeted Post as he emerged from the wreck turned out to be the Flat Mining Company's manager, and he had organized his men into a repair team. Since he worked for a mining company, he had at his disposal a full complement of tools. He told Post he called over the radio with the news of the crash and that Wiley's friend, Joe Crosson, radioed back and was bringing a new propeller and tools from Fairbanks. Crosson also persuaded Pan Am's chief mechanic, Loren Fernold, to accompany him.

When they arrived, Crosson and Post surveyed the damage and decided which repairs should be made on the spot and which ones could wait for Fairbanks, which boasted better facilities. While Crosson and the mechanics worked, Post went back to sleep.

By dawn, the *Winnie Mae* was air-worthy. Crosson lifted off through the patchy fog and Post followed. When they landed at Weeks Field in Fairbanks, Post said, "I want a bath, a shave, a big feed and some civilian clothes," while Crosson rounded up the best mechanics he could find, whether they worked for him or a rival airline. Post was a hero and everybody wanted to help. While Post slept, they swarmed over the plane, mending the landing gear, patching the fuselage, replacing a defective tube in the automatic direction finder, tuning the instruments, and replacing the tires.

While Post lost eight hours in Fairbanks and an entire night in Flat, on the bright side he was well rested and still ahead of his record. More important, his plane was in fine shape. He sped away from Fairbanks with Crosson's maps, but once again found himself battling the elements. At 21,000 feet over skyscraping mountains, the temperature in his cockpit plummeted to minus six and ice formed on the wings, forcing Post down at the rate of 100 feet a minute. He had the motor wide open, but his airspeed was only 125 mph and he couldn't correct his gradual descent. Cutting through thick clouds with 15,000-foot peaks in his path, he seriously considered fastening his parachute. Fortunately the weather improved at Whitehorse Junction in the Yukon.

After that it was smooth sailing. Post needed only 9 hours and 22 minutes to make Edmonton, arriving at Blatchford field in a driving rainstorm. Two years earlier with Gatty aboard Post had landed in a driving rainstorm. The runway was coated in mud, prompting Post to tell Gatty he wished the *Winnie Mae* had been mounted on floats. Taking off was dangerous. Post was afraid the ship could spin out. A Canadian mail pilot suggested they take off from Portage Avenue, a cleanly paved road that ran two miles from the airfield to town.

The mayor, aware of the international spotlight shining on his city, put emergency crews to work pulling down the electric light wires strung alongside the road. When Post revved the motor, mud splattered a crowd standing near the *Winnie Mae*. The plane sped down the road, electric light poles inches from its wing tips. Post floored it and the plane jumped to 75 mph until it lifted off the ground.

It was an awesome display of piloting skill. In some ways, Post's handicap was an advantage because he was accustomed to flying by feel and making instant calculations to compensate for his lack of depth perception. He often joked he would have to give up flying if they ever changed the height of two-story buildings. When they flew over the Hotel MacDonald, where they had stayed, the maître d'hôtel and his platoon of bellhops stood on the roof to offer a salute.

This time, 5000 people, many of whom had gathered through the night, were on hand to greet him. Post alit just long enough to ice his head, which ached from flying at high altitudes with insufficient oxygen, drink some ice water, catch a 30-minute nap, and refuel. Then he soared into the homestretch, 20 hours and 12 minutes ahead of his record. Next stop: New York, where, as *The Washington Post* wryly predicted, "Wiley Post's greatest ordeal will come when he lands among two hundred and fifty news photographers."

Post flew the final 2000 miles prodded by a stiff tailwind,

almost every mile tracked by an adoring public. He was first sighted ten miles northeast of Winnipeg. A forest ranger in a tower tagged him 28 miles north of Orr, Minnesota, in the northeast corner of that state at 5:45 p.m. He was spotted 30 miles west Lake Superior. Post crossed over Marquette, Michigan, on the south shore of the lake, at 7:50 p.m. The next report came from Toronto at 9:47 p.m. At 10:28 p.m. he was coming up on Niagara Falls.

Post amused himself by listening to radio coverage of his flight, which was the most enjoyable part of the trip. Yet he was disappointed he hadn't done better. He kicked himself for leaving a month after he should have—the weather for Mattern's flight had been far better. By his calculation he enjoyed three hours of clear weather the entire week. Even on this last leg, Post hurtled through smoky haze, evading two thunderstorms. Toward the end, he felt the crush of depression. Later, he confessed that he considered landing so he would arrive a day later and miss out on besting his record. Post dozed off several times after Toronto, letting the autopilot ease his burden.

A crowd of 75,000 massed early in the day at Brooklyn's Floyd Bennett Field while 5000 cars, bumper-to-bumper, clogged roads near and around the airport, resulting in the worst traffic jam in the city's history. As night fell, search-lights beamed above the field; at 9:35 p.m. a shrill whistle warned planes to keep clear until Post landed.

Harold Gatty, now an aerial navigation instructor and advisor to the United States Army, arrived in a bomber from Washington. "I am tickled to death at the prospect of Wiley beating our record," Gatty said. "After all he's gone through on this trip he certainly deserves it. It is just about the greatest flight ever, yet I am not surprised that he has come through. That's the kind of man and flier he is. I'll be right here on the ground waiting for him when he comes in."

The *Winnie Mae* swung over Newark airport, across the lower tip of Manhattan to Flatbush, Brooklyn. Post, arriving on a moonless night, had his motor throttled down so low that he was on top of Floyd Bennett Field before anyone saw him approach from the north 800 feet up.

Someone yelled, "There's a plane."

Lee Trenholm, Post's manager, sitting in a car with Mae Post and Harold Gatty, cried, "It must be Wiley!"

The cry spread like hot gossip. "It's Post! He's made it."

Earlier that day, Mae Post had posed for pictures, pretending to study a map of North America. "I think," she said, smiling, "that I would have to kill him if he tried it again." When a reporter reminded her she had said the same thing after Post's last world flight, she replied, "He had such perfect equipment for this flight and seemed so sure of success I agreed."

She had been asleep when word came in that Post had crashed at Flat. Trenholm kept the news from her until he was certain her husband was safe. Now that he was coming in, she could relax for the first time in months.

Airport officials were unprepared for Post's swift arrival. Minutes before they had received an erroneous report that he was 155 miles away in Pittston, PA, which meant he wouldn't reach Brooklyn for another hour. As a result, the floodlights were off until he began his descent. Switched on, the light beams shone on Post's white and purple plane for under a minute. There would be no broad circle for posterity as he had done last time. He set the *Winnie Mae* down gently.

The crowd erupted, and the 600 police were no match for the first wave of Post greeters. Post saw them coming and immediately turned his plane around and taxied 50 yards to the right in the hopes the police could regroup. Which they did. Officers on horseback and motorcycles repaired the foot patrolmen's broken ranks and pushed the crowd back. They formed a hollow square to protect the *Winnie Mae* and its pilot from the crush.

Philip D. Hoyt, first deputy police commissioner, was the first to reach the plane. As Post sat hunched up in the cockpit, Commissioner Hoyt reached up to shake hands. "Where have you been all week?" he asked.

"I couldn't tell you," Post said, a smile creasing his face.

Trenholm asked if he needed anything. Post said he was thirsty. Someone passed him a cup of water and he downed it in two gulps. A radio announcer pushed a microphone, and Post told his mother and father in Oklahoma he was tired but otherwise fine, and hoped they were all right, too. He handed the microphone back and sat still for 15 minutes, taking everything in. Finally, he flung open the hatch and scampered up and out, wearing the same gray trousers and blue shirt he wore when he left a week earlier. He was escorted through the crowd to a car, where his wife kissed him. At 12:20 a.m., they left the airport, escorted by a phalanx of motorcycle police, sirens blaring, to the Hotel Roosevelt.

There were days of celebration—a second tickertape up Broadway, where Post rode in a car alone as he had on his flight (plans for the *Winnie Mae* to join him were scuttled when it was learned her wingspan was too wide); a ceremony at City Hall: Post received a gold medal and attended banquets; and an appearance at the White House with Franklin Delano Roosevelt, who recounted some of Post's recent exploits to members of the Citizens' Military Training Corps.

With Post at his side, the President said, "I thought you'd like a chance to say 'howdy do' to the man who has just flown around the world. As of us Americans are proud of that little stunt of his going around the world in a little more than seven days." Then, playing on a theme relevant to his audience, he said, "It took not only a lot of courage and endurance but a lot of training. No one can pull off a thing like that without months of preparation. Millions of people were watching his progress and we are glad to welcome him back. At the same time we all feel just a little proud of the person who helped to make that trip possible, Mrs. Post."

Roosevelt asked the aviator to step up to the microphone. Post hesitated, but urged by Roosevelt, he said, "I admire the American uniform a great deal. I am sorry I have never worn it. I am proud to be here to talk to you." Then Roosevelt had Post share some adventures.

Afterward Post and his wife were scheduled to fly back to New York, but once again bad weather intervened.

They took the train instead.

CHAPTER 12

Even When He Loses, He Wins

JIMMIE MATTERN ESCAPED NOME TO JOIN HIS RESCUE group just as Wiley Post was one hop from New York. The capacious *Bellanca*, equipped with a miniscule 225 horsepower engine, was sitting on an abbreviated runway. Mattern unloaded every pound he could do without, yet still barely cleared the trees surrounding the field. He made it to Prince George—about halfway to Edmonton—and stopped for the night.

The next morning he experienced another stressful take off. The runway was muddy and short, and Mattern frantically pulled back on the stick. As soon as he left a wall of trees in his stead the engine stalled. The *Bellanca* fluttered to earth like a duck struck by buckshot. Lucky for Mattern, there was a valley beyond the trees, and he managed to right the ship and convince the engine to restart before he hit the ground.

He flew to Edmonton, where he picked up yet another ship, which promptly blew a gasket en route to Buffalo. Mattern took a car to Toronto and borrowed another plane. He wondered if "someone was trying to tell me something." In Buffalo, Ed Aldrin parked a Lockheed Vega, with an eagle much like the one on his *Century of Progress* painted on the side. It was full of radio equipment, and as Mattern was flying over the George Washington Bridge he gave the first air-to-ground international broadcast.

As he buzzed Floyd Bennett Field in Brooklyn, Mattern sobbed in his cockpit. How many times had he wondered if he would ever see that airport again? Soon after, he touched down at 4:41 p.m. on July 31, 1933, ten days after Post arrived, on the same runway from which he had left. He didn't break the round-the-world speed record or best his friendly rival, "but I beat Magellan by a few days," Mattern said. The "Robinson Crusoe of the air," as *The New York Times* dubbed him, 15 pounds lighter than when he had taken off from New York, emerged from the ship to resounding cheers from a small but boisterous crowd. Wearing Russian boots and limping, the young flier stepped forward to shake hands.

During a ceremony at City Hall before 5,000 people, Mayor James P. O'Brien congratulated Mattern on his safe return, "notwithstanding the many mishaps and obstacles which you met and surmounted. One cannot but marvel at the youthful pluck and determination which enabled you to survive this memorable flight—the consummation of a well-designed plan for a continuous round-the-world dash is a subject of great glory and acclaim, but more glorious still, in my humble opinion, is the surmounting and conquest of unforeseen continuous setbacks and difficulties."

The City Hall ceremony was just the beginning. Tributes in Washington and Cleveland, and Jimmie Mattern Day at the Chicago Worlds Fair followed, as well as celebrations in Milwaukee, Kansas City, St. Louis, Oklahoma City, and San Angelo, his hometown. When it was all over Mattern checked into a hotel and "established new non-stop sleeping records."

Through failure, Mattern became a bigger celebrity than if he had actually succeeded. After visiting the White House he opened a two-week engagement at New York's Paramount Theater, earning an eye-popping $17,000 a week—roughly $250,000 a week in today's dollars. Audiences lined up to hear his stories of surviving the Arctic tundra until Eskimos rescued him. He followed that with another two weeks at Chicago's State and Lake Theater. Mattern forgot flying for a while and lived the high life, moving into a suite at the Sherman Hotel in the Loop in Chicago.

The following year he starred on a radio show, sponsored by the Pure Oil Company, that dramatized his life. During its run, Mattern embellished much of his early life for the sake of entertainment. He claimed he had served in the U.S. Army Air Corps and graduated as his class's top cadet, rescued a woman and her baby who were trapped in a forest fire, went on tour with a famous wing walker who died after jumping from his plane, worked as a private pilot for a wealthy businessman in Hawaii, and increased the number of films he worked on as a stunt pilot from one to three. Mattern never exaggerated his round-the-world flying adventures and Siberian crash landing, though. These needed no doctoring. The company pumped $1 million into the development of the show, called *The Diary of Jimmie Mattern*. Seventy-two stations across the nation carried it five nights a week for 23 weeks.

Mattern rode out the next few years of the Great Depression dating starlets and chorus girls, and hobnobbing with the rich and famous, including Will Rogers, who never met an airman he didn't like. During this time Mattern met a showgirl named Dorothy. Before he could marry her, however, he needed to divorce Delia, who had long ago settled in Walla Walla. In his divorce action in Chicago, he charged her with abandonment, which must have been a bitter pill for her to swallow. In his unpublished autobiography, which he wrote a few years before he died, he scrubbed any mention of her from of its pages. The divorce was granted in 1937, and Mattern married Dorothy the next day. They would be together for more than 50 years.

Later that year Mattern proposed another solo round-the-world trip—this time he planned to refuel in mid-air—but Soviet authorities denied him a visa. Instead the Russian ambassador asked Mattern to join the search for the missing Levanevsky, the pilot who had dropped Mattern off in Nome from Anadyr and was reported missing between Barrow, Alaska, and the North Pole.

It would be a fruitless search. Levanevsky's body wouldn't be found for another 50 years.

CHAPTER 13

Fatal Error

AFTER RETURNING TO OKLAHOMA, WILEY POST TRIED to capitalize on his fame with a cross-country promotional tour sponsored by an oil company. His first stop was Quincy, Illinois, but right after take off, his engine cut out at 50 feet above the ground and Post lost control. The *Winnie Mae* dropped from the sky and crashed into a fence. The cockpit was a crumpled mess and Post suffered a fractured skull. Almost immediately souvenir hunters gathered up pieces of the plane while Post was taken to a nearby hospital, where he convalesced for more than a week.

During this period, Post wallowed in depression, a condition that had bedeviled him his entire life. Almost immediately after accomplishing something, he would wonder, *Is this all there is?* He was a man more comfortable in motion than at rest. But there were bills to pay and he never could capitalize on his exploits—certainly not at the level of Lindbergh or Amelia Earhart, who went on the lecture circuit, designed her own line of active wear clothing, and wrote articles. In contrast, Post was naturally shy, didn't have the gift of gab, and was far more at home in his plane than in front of any audience.

Post considered other aerial distance records, but none seemed as compelling as the one he had just completed. The only direction he could go, he reasoned, was straight up, which, he theorized, could dramatically increase his top speed. The key, or so he postulated, would be to fly in the substratosphere—somewhere between 30,000 and 40,000 feet above the earth, where air was lighter and a plane could travel faster while consuming less fuel. To do it, he would need to break altitude records.

That meant he had to find a way to breathe far above the earth. Through experience, he knew that the Earth's atmosphere thins the higher the altitude. At 15,000 feet, air is only one-half as dense as it is at sea level; at 30,000 feet the pressure is so low and the level of oxygen so small that humans can't survive. If Post could figure out a way to soar far above the clouds, fierce weather would be far less dangerous. But the *Winnie Mae*, made of wood, was not a candidate for pressurizing. If he couldn't seal his plane, he'd seal himself.

In 1934, bankrolled by Frank Phillips of the Phillips Petroleum Company, Post worked with Russell S. Colley of the B.F. Goodrich Company to develop what became the world's first practical pressure suit. The first prototype didn't fit because Post had put on weight. A second suit was created, but it became rigid and immobile when pressurized. Post couldn't move inside the inflated suit, much less work the controls of the plane. Many attempts later, they came up with a design that worked. The suit was pressurized by his airplane engine's supercharger and had three layers: long underwear, an inner black rubber air pressure bladder, and an outer suit constructed of rubberized parachute fabric.

The outer suit was glued to a frame with arm and leg joints so that he could operate the flight controls and move about the aircraft. Attached were pigskin gloves, rubber boots, and a scuba diver's helmet, which had a removable faceplate that could be sealed and was equipped with earphones and a microphone. To provide visibility, Colley built in a small viewing port—a larger one was unnecessary because Post only had one eye. When he wore it, he looked like a cross between the Michelin Man and a Cyclops.

In his first flight in the new suit on September 5, 1934, Post achieved an altitude of 40,000 feet above Chicago. Eventually he flew as high as 50,000 feet, although this was an unofficial record because one of the onboard barographs, which measures altitude, froze at 35,000 feet, and the National Aeronautic Association of U.S.A refused to certify the height, even though the other altimeter onboard confirmed Post's claim.

It was during these high altitude record-setting missions that Post discovered the jet stream—a river of fast-moving air at high altitudes that flows from west to east. Not only was the air thinner up there, cutting down on drag, the winds actually pushed the aircraft along. To cut down on wind resistance, Post rigged up a system so he could drop his landing gear immediately after takeoff. When he got to New York, he planned to land on a special skid attached to the plane's underbelly.

Before dawn on February 22, 1935, a crowd of reporters, photographers, and National Aeronautical Association officials gathered at Burbank airport and watched Will Rogers help Post into his pressure suit. About 20 feet off the ground, Post dropped his landing gear and the *Winnie Mae* shot skyward. It took Post 35 minutes to reach 24,000 feet, and then he started cruising eastward. He had covered only 225 miles when an oil line burst. With no way to unload the 300 gallons of fuel on board, he cut the engine and glided to earth, making a perfect landing on Muroc Dry Lake. The only causality: a bent propeller blade. Post climbed out of the *Winnie Mae* and sought help.

The L*os Angeles Chronicle* reported what happened next. An unsuspecting motorist with engine trouble had his head under the hood when he felt a hand on his shoulder. He looked up and "screamed in terror. Before him stood a weird apparition with a head encased in a huge helmet out of which stared a great glass eye." Afraid that monsters from Mars were attacking, the motorist tried to flee. "I had a time calming him down but I finally succeeded and he helped me out of my oxygen helmet," Post told the *Chronicle*. The two then went to a telegraph office for help.

This experience added to the Wiley Post legend. Will Rogers, a big booster of aviation in the 1930s, wrote in his column: "Was out at daybreak to see Wiley Post take off. Was in the camera plane and we flew along with him for about thirty miles. We left him 8,000 feet over the mountains. He soon after had to land. He brought her down on her stomach. That guy don't need wheels."

It turned out it wasn't a leaky oil hose that had grounded Post. It was sabotage. Someone had poured two pounds of steel shavings and powdered emery into the *Winnie Mae*'s engine, which caused the engine to overheat. An investigation never identified a culprit, although Post believed it was a rival pilot determined to see him fail.

While in California, Wiley Post appeared in a Warner Bros. film, *Air Hawks*. The plot: A mysterious ray immobilizes all motors and engines and threatens the nation's security. Although he was listed high in the credits, Post was on screen for only a few moments.

By March 1935, Post took off with a rebuilt engine on another attempt at a cross-country flight on the jet stream. He made 2000 miles in 7 hours and 19 minutes, averaging 279 mph, 100 mph faster than the plane's maximum speed. However, a malfunction in his pressure suit caused oxygen to flow into his helmet, fogging his eyepiece and making him groggy. Unable to use his hands to clear away the fog, he used the end of his nose, and aborted the flight in Cleveland. Although he failed, he had made his point. Just as he predicted, pilots in the not-so-distant future would ride the jet stream coast-to-coast at unprecedented speeds, completing the trip in hours instead of days.

Post retired the *Winnie Mae* once and for all and wondered how he would earn a living. For all his fame, he never seemed to have enough money. He began planning what would turn out to be his final trip.

At first he wanted to take his wife, Mae, but she didn't want to go. Mrs. Charles Lindbergh might have taken flying lessons and accompanied her husband to the farthest reaches of the globe but Mae Post would just as soon stay home. Post invited Fay Gillis, the aviatrix who had helped him in Siberia on his solo round-the-world journey. After accepting, she had to back out when famed journalist Linton Wells proposed and they eloped to Ethiopia to cover the war. Post figured if he had to go alone, he would.

He approached Pan Am for financial assistance, and after mapping out the route offered his services as a company pilot. But Pan Am believed that stunt pilots like Post were good for front-page news but too unreliable to work as steady pilots: They were likely to go off in pursuit of another record. Lyman Peck, Pan Am's director of Alaskan development, tried to soften the blow by pointing Post to Will Rogers' weekly article of March 10, 1935: "I never been to that Alaska," Rogers wrote. "I am crazy to go up there some time."

Post decided to have a talk with his friend. It would be a fateful decision.

Will Rogers, star of stage, screen, and newspaper, was the biggest entertainer of his generation, commanding an annual salary in excess of $1 million at a time when the average wage was 50 cents an hour. He could hold the attention of a sold-out crowd at Carnegie Hall by merely dangling his legs from the stage and talking off the cuff. But he was more than just a star. He had become an American cultural icon, who, like Post, had risen up from the prairie to become household name.

Rogers and Post met in the mid-1920s when Post gave him a lift in his plane, and as Oklahomans connected by upbringing they became fast friends. At the same time, Rogers was a strong advocate of aviation before it became the industry it is today. Although he got airsick every time he got in a plane, he flew hundreds of thousands of miles every year, and dedicated numerous columns to flight. By the time 1935 rolled around, he wanted a break. When Post approached him with his idea, Rogers gave it a lot of thought. His wife didn't want him to go, but he convinced her she could join the two men in Europe.

Tight on money, Post mixed and matched parts to create his own "bastard" plane, with a wing from a used Lockheed Explorer and the body from a Lockheed Orion 9-E Special. He added pontoons because he expected to take off and land mostly in water in Alaska and Siberia. The plane was ugly. Lockheed viewed it as a "freak," and refused to put its stamp of approval on it. It was also nose-heavy, which Post counteracted by pulling back on the stick. Joe Crosson, who Post regarded as a peer, flatly told him the plane wasn't safe and he shouldn't fly it. But Post stubbornly believed in his piloting skills, and after several test runs was confident he could handle it.

While Post supplied the plane, Rogers paid for everything else, and the two set off for Alaska, camping, fishing, and hunting whenever the urge struck them. Along the way, Rogers continued to type his weekly columns. Most of them covered his adventures in Alaska. In his final column he related a story he had heard from a gold miner. It involved a bear and a dog and a rifle. The last word he typed was "death."

At 11:30 a.m. on August 15, 1935, Post and Rogers climbed into the plane, which was docked on the Chena River. Once Post taxied to the center of the waterway, he turned the plane to face the wind and burst forward, climbing rapidly until he disappeared over the trees. One of the pilots standing near a communications superintendent for Alaska Airways commented that with a takeoff like that, if the engine quit, Post would be a goner. This type of hotdog flying was unheard of for a floatplane. What's more, Post hadn't bothered to check the weather in Barrow, where a thick fog bank was rolling in.

At 7:30 p.m. Post was lost and near the end of his fuel supply. He dropped down low enough to spot a small camp of Native Americans and landed to ask directions. The Okpeaha family was surprised when a plane splashed to a stop nearby, and even more surprised when two men emerged. Post asked directions and the father, Claire Okpeaha, pointed lazily to the north and said in broken English that Barrow was about 30 miles away. Rogers asked how the hunting had been. Good, the man replied: walrus, seal, caribou, enough food for the winter. Post and Rogers stretched their legs and discussed the situation. The fog made it hard to see where they were going, but Barrow—and a warm bed and hot meal—stood a few minutes away. They decided to go for it.

Post jumpstarted the engine and zoomed across the water, rising steeply and banking sharply. At 400 feet, the engine backfired and the plane stalled in mid-air. It somersaulted straight down, the nose hitting the shallow water, driving the motor halfway up through the cabin, the right wing shearing off, shattering the floats. The plane fell on its back with the water covering the upside-down fuselage and engine.

The only sounds were the wind sweeping over the tundra and the sizzling sound of the hot steel engine in the icy water.

Claire Okpeaha ran to the water's edge, calling out "Halloo, halloo!"

There was no answer.

CHAPTER 14

Funeral for Two Friends

SOMETIME AFTER MIDNIGHT, A RINGING TELEPHONE WOKE Jimmie Mattern from a sound sleep. "Jimmie, this is United Press. Have you heard the news?"

"Have I heard what?"

"Will Rogers and Wiley Post were killed last night, in their airplane. It crashed up near Point Barrow, Alaska."

Mattern asked him to repeat it. As he listened he sat on the edge of his bed, numb and wondering if there could be a mistake. Then another thought looped through his head. He had almost taken Rogers on that flight. Would things have ended differently?

At 6 a.m. the phone nudged Joe Crosson awake. He padded into the kitchen followed by his wife, Lillian, picked up the receiver, listened without saying a word, hung up, and told his wife what happened. Then he went into the bathroom and got sick.

When Mae Post learned what had happened, she wailed, "I wish to God I had been with him when he crashed." Post's mother recalled the last time she had seen her son, before his fourth and final unsuccessful attempt at a trans-continental trek on the jet stream. "Son, do be careful, but we hope you make good and that everything comes out right this time," she had said. He replied, "I'll do my best."

Word came too late to make the regular newspaper edition, so extras were printed, with newsboys trumpeting the shocking news. The nation's flags flew at half-staff. Charles Lindbergh paid to have the bodies flown back to Oklahoma, and Joe Crosson was the one who would do the flying. His wife begged him to find someone else for the trip. She was worried he was too distraught to make the journey from Alaska to Oklahoma, but Crosson insisted.

After the bodies were brought to Barrow by boat, a local physician worked through the night to realign limbs and suture the massive wounds. During the crash the motor had driven straight into Post and his intestines had spilled out. Will Rogers's skull had been crushed. Although Crosson was known for never taking unnecessary risks, he rushed off in a heavy fog, flying low over the Cadillac River with near zero visibility. His co-pilot later said he was "scared" the entire journey, because he thought Crosson was "trying to do too much."

While Crosson made his way to Fairbanks, his wife received Post and Rogers' personal effects, which were delivered to her. Their wallets were still wet, so she placed them by the cook stove where two days earlier she had prepared their last home-cooked meal. That's when Post and Rogers had stayed overnight. From Rogers' wallet she recognized family photos he showed her, and she began to weep.

Crosson rested in Fairbanks, and Pacific Alaska Airways mechanics prepared a Lockheed Electra for the flight to Seattle, the next stop on the journey. Meanwhile, a funeral home worked on the bodies and put them in coffins that were loaded onboard. En route, Crosson received a message from Juan Trippe, owner of Pan Am, Alaska Airways' parent company. Trippe ordered Crosson to land in Vancouver, not Seattle, where they would stay overnight.

Crosson couldn't understand why Trippe had changed the schedule, until he learned he would be changing planes again—this time to a DC-2, Pan Am's newest and the most impressive-looking plane in its fleet. *Pan American Airways* was painted in bright red letters on the side. Trippe needed the extra day to scrounge up a DC-2 up from Texas to Seattle so that newspapers and newsreels would have no choice but to give the airline free publicity. Crosson was upset Trippe made the world wait an extra day for a publicity stunt.

Post's funeral was held in the First Baptist Church in Sentinel, Oklahoma. It was a simple service—as simple as Wiley Post the man. Jimmie Mattern and Joe Crosson attended together, with Crosson flying back to Chicago with his friend. Along the way Crosson filled Mattern in on the details of Post's crash.

When the funeral service was over, the church was cleared of everyone except family members, who spent a final few minutes with their dead. Then the coffin was placed in a hearse. Thousands rushed to follow it on its way to the cemetery. Overhead planes dropped flowers. The procession ended at Fairlawn's Mausoleum, where Wiley Post's body was interred, marked with a simple, unassuming headstone. In New York City, pilots gathered in the skies, and a squadron of 24 planes flew over Floyd Bennett Field, Manhattan, and back to Brooklyn.

Will Rogers' funeral was the largest one in Oklahoma history. And in Hollywood, 20,000 people joined for a special ceremony. *The Herald Tribune* summed it up: "Will Rogers hadn't a living peer in the affection of millions, and Wiley Post ranked next to Lindbergh as their hero of the air."

EPILOGUE

L IKE MANY WHO KNEW WILEY POST, JIMMIE MATTERN was not satisfied with the findings of the official government investigation of the crash, which blamed "engine trouble." After Post's funeral, Joe Crosson and Mattern spent hours deconstructing the accident. Crosson told Mattern that Post had ordered pontoons, but the ones that arrived were designed for a Fokker Trimotor—a much bigger plane. Impatient to get moving, Post used them anyway, even though they accentuated his plane's nose heaviness. After buzzing around the world twice, he had an almost supernatural belief in his own immortality. He told Crosson he had the skill to keep the old girl under control.

Two years later Mattern found himself up in Alaska, where he had joined the search for Sigismund Levanevsky, whose plane, it was believed, had gone down somewhere between Barrow, Alaska, and the North Pole. Before taking to the air, Mattern stopped in on Charlie Brower, an Alaskan folk hero that Rogers had been keen to meet. Brower, known as "King of the Arctic," had lived on Alaska's northern coast for 50 years as a trader and whaler. In the process, he had become a very wealthy man. He married an Eskimo woman, and after she died he married another one. Brower was the chief of police and federal government's local magistrate.

He took Mattern to meet the last man to see Post and Rogers alive. Claire Okpeaha, with Brower translating, described their final minutes: "We watched from the shore. We heard the motor rev up to a deafening pitch and saw the plane begin moving, faster, faster, pontoons spraying behind as the plane came up on the steps of the floats. Lifting off and starting to climb, it banked to the right, making a turn toward Barrow."

Mattern thought, *Of course Ol' Wiley banked to the right. He only had one eye. But with a nose-heavy plane and an engine that had been cooling for ten minutes, that would have been an extremely risky maneuver.*

The Inuit continued: "Suddenly the engine misfired and sputtered. The plane's nose went down and it hurtled into the shallow lagoon and flipped over on its back. There was a dull explosion, a flash of fire and then dead silence. Our first instinct was to run away. Then I went a little closer. I went as close as I could and shouted over and over but got no answer."

Okpeaha left the others to gape at the wreckage while he ran 12 miles through tundra grass and around lagoons to get to Charlie Brower. Five hours later he collapsed at Brower's feet, so out of breath he could hardly speak. Finally he got out "crash," "one man big have tall boots, other man have sore eye, rag over eye," and Brower knew immediately who he was talking about.

Mattern shook his head. As a pilot, Post was like a cowboy on a bucking bronco. He was confident he could handle any situation in any airplane. And Rogers was relentlessly restless and had complete faith in Post. He believed his friend could fly to Mars, if need be. But the truth was, that "bastard" plane of Wiley's should have never left the ground. Post's style of banking hard to the right on takeoff was fine in a sleek Lockheed Vega, but was precisely the wrong approach to take in a low-wing plane like the one he had mashed together from odd parts. Before he took off, the wet fog would have caused condensation in the carburetor. In a steep bank, the nose-heavy plane would simply stall out with no chance to recover.

Charlie Brower presented Mattern with the seatbelts that hugged Post and Rogers when they died, as well as the plane's throttle and some papers Will Rogers had on him.

In 1935 everyone knew of this crash but few knew the circumstances which created this tragedy, Mattern wrote in his diary.

They are not forgotten. They were my friends.

Beyond

Wiley Post, along with Will Rogers, is commemorated with two monuments at the crash site in Barrow, Alaska, which are listed on the National Register of Historic Places. A small airfield in Oklahoma City is named after Post, while the major commercial airport is named after Will Rogers. Post received the Distinguished Flying Cross in 1932 and the Gold Medal of Belgium and International Harmon Trophy in 1934. In an interesting bit of synchronicity, the *Winnie Mae*'s license expired the very day Wiley Post perished in Alaska.

The Smithsonian Museum purchased the *Winnie Mae* for $25,000 from Post's wife after his death in 1936. Mae Post took the money and bought a small cotton farm in Texas, where she lived the rest of her life. She never remarried and always wore the wedding band her beloved "Weeley" gave her. A portrait of her late husband hung on a wall in her living room across from a photo of Post and Will Rogers taken just before the crash. In 1969 Wiley Post was enshrined in the National Aviation Hall of Fame, and ten years later the U.S. Post Office issued two commemorative airmail stamps bearing his likeness. As the years have worn on, however, he is best known as a character who pops up throughout the Broadway revue *Will Rogers Follies*, with one recurring line: "Let's go flyin'!" Rogers does, and the play ends.

Jimmie Mattern returned to flying, joining Lockheed in 1938 to test pilot the P-38, which had been killing an alarming number of trainee pilots. He developed a dual control system for the experimental craft so an instructor could take over at any time, dramatically lowering the accident rate. In 1946, afflicted by spasms and shakes, Mattern was diagnosed with a ruptured blood vessel in his brain from too many vertiginous dives from high altitudes. Doctors gave him only a few years to live. They were off by more than 40. But he never flew again. Lockheed removed him from the payroll when he couldn't return to the air. When he asked the company to cover medical expenses, Lockheed claimed it could open the company up to lawsuits and refused.

He and his wife, Dorothy, moved to Phoenix and became licensed real estate brokers and opened a travel agency, while Mattern operated as an aviation consultant. Buzz Aldrin carried Mattern's pilot's license (signed by Orville Wright) to the moon on Apollo XI. Jimmie Mattern died on December 17, 1988, two days before he was to be the honoree at Texas Aviation Pioneer Day.

Harold Gatty worked for Pan Am as a South Pacific representative after his globetrotting days ended. During WWII he was a Royal Australian Air Force captain and consultant to the U.S. Army. Many GIs who were forced down credited Gatty's slender volume *The Raft Book* with saving their lives. It offered tips on using the flight paths of birds, as well as observing weather patterns, vegetation, shifting sands, patterns of snow fields, and the positions of the sun, moon and stars to navigate unfamiliar terrain. He moved to Fiji to become an owner of Fiji Airlines, and at 54 died of a heart attack on Aug. 30, 1957.

Bennett H. Griffin became an aeronautical inspector after returning home with Jimmie Mattern in 1932, and then served as a major in the Air Force during World War II. In 1940 he landed the first plane at the new National Airport in Washington, DC, and took over as the director in 1947, where over the next decade he watched the number of take-offs and landings during his ten-year tenure quadruple to about 4 million in 1957. When he retired from consulting in 1973 the National Aeronautics Association named him a "Distinguished Elder Statesman of American Aviation." He died on April 28, 1978.

THE END

Photo Gallery

Wiley Post and Harold Gatty in a ticker tape
parade up Broadway, 1931

Levanevsky and Mattern near Nome, Alaska

Autographed photo of Wiley Post

Mattern hailed on his return

Wiley Post's pilot's license

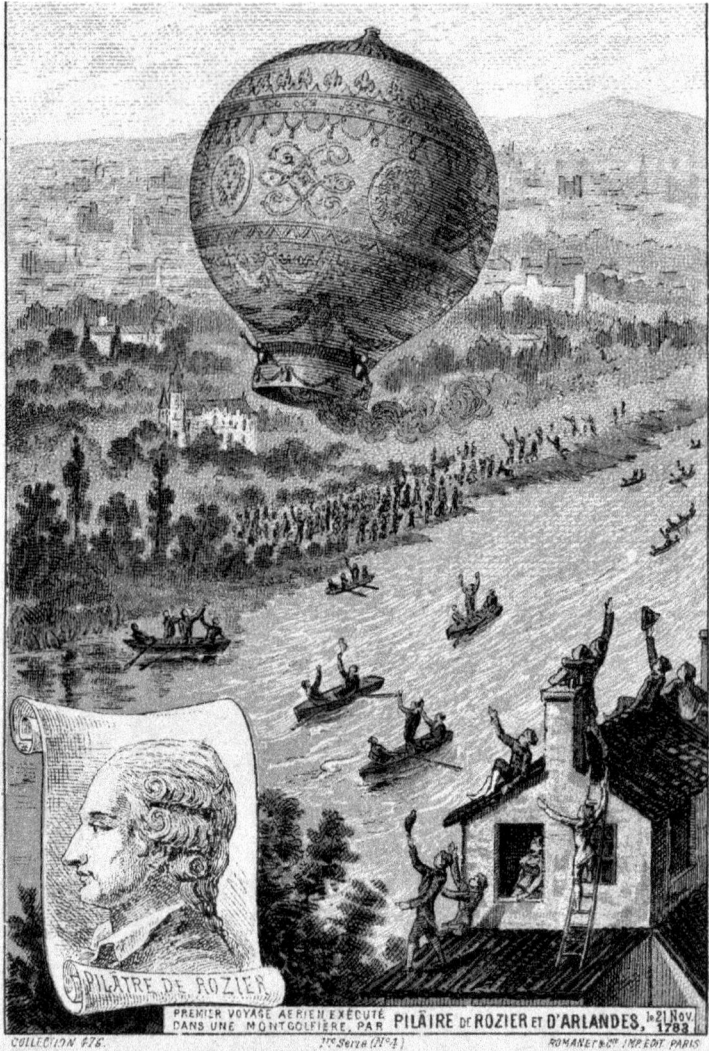

The first hot air balloon flight

Orville Wright and the Wright Flyer, 1909

Wiley and Mae Post posing for newspaper photograph

Mattern in the news

The crash of the *Winnie Mae*

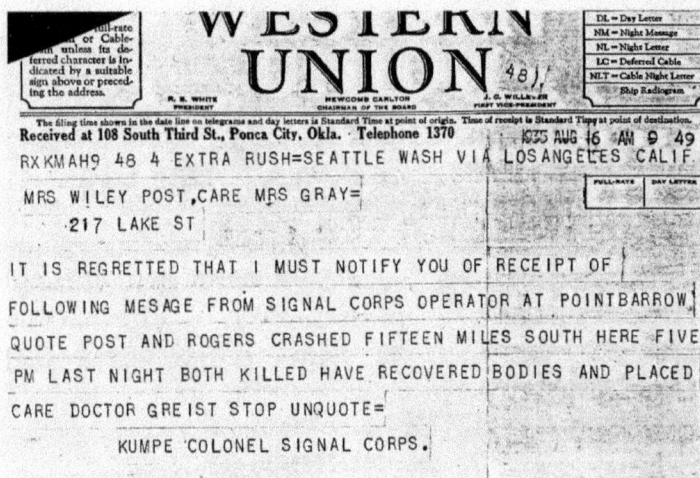

Western Union telegram informing Mae Post of Wiley's death.

Telegram announcing the deaths of Post and Rogers

Mattern just prior to take-off, 1933

Amelia Earhart and Wiley Post

Wiley Post and Charles Lindbergh (center)

One of the last photos of Rogers and Post

AUTHOR'S NOTE

THIS IS THE STORY OF TWO FORGOTTEN HEROES WHO RISKED life and limb to become the first solo pilot to circumnavigate the world.

A narrative involving two long-dead people offers great challenges to a writer. It's not like you can dash off an email or pick up the phone to ask questions. Yet every word in *Sky Rivals* is true. All dialogue, anecdotes, and characters' internal thoughts come from the subjects themselves, through their own writings and via press coverage.

In 1933, when this story takes place, they were both as famous as any men alive, their exploits splashed in screaming, jumbo-font newspaper headlines and used as fodder for newsreels. In addition to the voluminous newspaper coverage – literally hundreds of news articles – they dictated columns for *The New York Times* describing the details of their flights while they were en route, and in their lifetimes gave dozens of interviews.

Wiley Post, the one-eyed pilot from Oklahoma, co-authored a book, *Around The World in Eight Days*, which described his first global circumnavigation with a navigator in 1931, and has been the subject of several biographies. Jimmie Mattern penned a series of short books, much, but not all apocryphal, to promote his coast-to-coast radio show. Before he died, he set the record straight in his unpublished memoirs, including a diary he kept. I attained a copy through the University of Texas at Dallas library.

In addition to hundreds of newspaper and magazine articles, I relied on the following sources:

Will Rogers & Wiley Post: Death at Barrow, by Bryan B. Sterling and Frances N. Sterling, M Evans & Co., 1993.

From Oklahoma to Eternity: The Life of Wiley Post and the Winnie Mae, by Bob Burke, Kenny Arthur Franks and Gini Moore Campbell, Oklahoma Heritage Association, 1998.

Around The World In Eight Days, by Wiley Post, Crown, 1989 (originally published in 1932).

Forgotten Eagle: Wiley Post, America's Heroic Aviation Pioneer, by Bryan B. Sterling and Frances N. Sterling, Carroll & Graf Publishers, 2001.

Fay Gillis Wells in the Air and On the Air, by Lillian Brinnon and Howard Fried, Woodfield Press, 2002.

Around the World in 80 Years Paperback, by Arthur Post (Wiley Post's brother), self-published, unknown date.

Cloud Country (Book 1): Wings of Youth, by Jimmie Mattern, Pure Oil Company, 1936.

Cloud Country (Book 2): Hawaii to Hollywood, Pure Oil Company, 1936.

Cloud Country (Book 3): Lost in Siberia, Pure Oil Company, 1936.

The Diary of Jimmie Mattern, Pioneer Airman (unpublished autobiography), 1991 (courtesy of the James J. "Jimmie" Mattern Collection, History of Aviation Collection, Special Collections Department, McDermott Library, The University of Texas at Dallas.

Mercy Pilot: The Joe Crosson Story, Epicenter Press, 2002.

Fifty Years Below Zero: A Lifetime of Adventure in the Far North, by Charles Brower, University of Alaska Press, 1994.

I owe a debt of gratitude to Atavist, the multimedia publisher, for publishing a significantly shorter version of this book under the title *Cloud Racers*, and Dorothy Zemach, editor of Wayzgoose Press, for creating this paperback and ebook.

Adam L. Penenberg
Brooklyn, NY
2016

ABOUT THE AUTHOR

Adam L. Penenberg is a journalism professor at New York University who has written for *Fast Company*, *Forbes*, the *New York Times*, the *Washington Post*, *Wired*, *Slate*, *Playboy*, and the *Economist*. A former senior editor at Forbes and a reporter for Forbes.com, Penenberg garnered national attention in 1998 for unmasking serial fabricator Stephen Glass of the *New Republic*. Penenberg's story was a watershed for online investigative journalism and portrayed in the film *Shattered Glass* (Steve Zahn plays Penenberg).

Penenberg has published several books that have been optioned for film and serialized in the *New York Times Magazine*, *Wired UK*, and the *Financial Times*, and won a Deadline Club Award for feature reporting for his *Fast Company* story "Revenge of the Nerds," which looked at the future of movie-making. He has appeared on NBC's The Today Show as well as on CNN and all the major news networks, and has been quoted about media and technology in the *Washington Post*, the *Christian Science Monitor*, *USA Today*, *Wired News*, *Ad Age*, *Marketwatch*, *Politico*, and many others.

He released two novels in 2012, *Virtually True*, the Independent Publisher (IPPY) silver award winner for science fiction, 2014, and *Trial & Terror*, both published by Wayzgoose Press.

His non-fiction print titles include *Play at Work: How Games Inspire Breakthrough Thinking*, *Viral Loop: From Facebook to Twitter, How Today's Smartest Businesses Grow Themselves*, and *Blood Highways: The True Story behind the*

Ford-Firestone Killing Machine.

Recently, Adam's article *The Troll's Lawyer* was voted as a Longreads #1 story for 2015.

His website is www.penenberg.com.